D0447249

Love...

What's Personality
Got to Do with It?

May epur
life be filled
with joy and your
heart filled with
love... Light-Love~
Carol

Also by Carol Ritberger

What Color Is Your Personality?

Your Personality, Your Health

Hay House Titles of Related Interest

Dating Disasters and How to Avoid Them, by Dr. Joy Browne

Feng Shui Dos & Taboos for Love, by Angi Ma Wong

The Love Book, by John Randolph Price

Love Notes (book-with-CD),
by Jim Brickman and Cindy Pearlman

Mars/Venus Cards, by John Gray

A Relationship for a Lifetime, by Kelly E. Johnson, M.D.

Secrets of Attraction, by Sandra Anne Taylor

All of the above are available at your
local bookstore, or may be ordered by visiting:
Hay House USA: **www.hayhouse.com**
Hay House Australia: **www.hayhouse.com.au**
Hay House UK: **www.hayhouse.co.uk**
Hay House South Africa: **orders@psdprom.co.za**

Love...

What's Personality Got to Do with It?

Working at Love to Make Love Work

Carol Ritberger, Ph.D.

HAY HOUSE, INC.
Carlsbad, California
London • Sydney • Johannesburg
Vancouver • Hong Kong

Copyright © 2006 by Carol Ritberger

Published and distributed in the United States by: Hay House, Inc., P.O. Box 5100, Carlsbad, CA 92018-5100 • *Phone:* (760) 431-7695 or (800) 654-5126 • *Fax:* (760) 431-6948 or (800) 650-5115 • www.hayhouse.com • **Published and distributed in Australia by:** Hay House Australia Pty. Ltd., 18/36 Ralph St., Alexandria NSW 2015 • *Phone:* 612-9669-4299 • *Fax:* 612-9669-4144 • www.hayhouse.com.au • **Published and distributed in the United Kingdom by:** Hay House UK, Ltd. • Unit 62, Canalot Studios • 222 Kensal Rd., London W10 5BN • *Phone:* 44-20-8962-1230 • *Fax:* 44-20-8962-1239 • www.hayhouse.co.uk • **Published and distributed in the Republic of South Africa by:** Hay House SA (Pty), Ltd., P.O. Box 990, Witkoppen 2068 • *Phone/Fax:* 27-11-706-6612 • orders@psdprom.co.za • **Distributed in Canada by:** Raincoast • 9050 Shaughnessy St., Vancouver, B.C. V6P 6E5 • *Phone:* (604) 323-7100 • *Fax:* (604) 323-2600

Editorial supervision: Jill Kramer • *Design:* Tricia Breidenthal

All rights reserved. No part of this book may be reproduced by any mechanical, photographic, or electronic process, or in the form of a phonographic recording; nor may it be stored in a retrieval system, transmitted, or otherwise be copied for public or private use—other than for "fair use" as brief quotations embodied in articles and reviews—without prior written permission of the publisher.

The author of this book does not dispense medical advice or prescribe the use of any technique as a form of treatment for physical or medical problems without the advice of a physician, either directly or indirectly. The intent of the author is only to offer information of a general nature to help you in your quest for emotional and spiritual well-being. In the event you use any of the information in this book for yourself, which is your constitutional right, the author and the publisher assume no responsibility for your actions.

Library of Congress Cataloging-in-Publication Data

Ritberger, Carol.
  Love--what's personality got to do with it? : working at love to make love work / Carol Ritberger.
     p. cm.
  Includes bibliographical references.
  ISBN-13: 978-1-4019-0568-2 (tradepaper)
  ISBN-10: 1-4019-0568-4 (tradepaper)
  1. Love--Miscellanea. 2. Typology (Psychology) 3. Color--Psychological aspects.
4. Personality--Miscellanea. I. Title.
  BF575.L8R58 2006
  152.4'1--dc22
                              2005007693

                    ISBN 13: 978-1-4019-0568-2
                    ISBN 10: 1-4019-0568-4

                  09 08 07 06   4 3 2 1
                    1st printing, January 2006

          Printed in the United States of America

To the love of my life—my husband, Bruce.

*Thank you for being the most loving,
inspirational, and encouraging partner
any Yellow personality could ever ask for.
And thanks for all the years of learning how
relationships should work, might work,
and don't work. Two Yellows living
together is a continual adventure.*

I love loving you.

Editor's note: In order to avoid awkward "he/she," "him/her" construc-
tions, we have often used the plural "they" or "their" to refer to singular
antecedents such as "mate" or "spouse."

Contents

Introduction

Another Book about Love?

As I searched through an endless number of bookstores and Websites gathering research materials for this project, I repeatedly asked myself, *Why am I writing another book about love?* There are certainly more than enough currently available. Yet I persevered despite my reservations, because it's the number one topic of interest to anyone seeking—or currently involved in—a romantic relationship.

The more I read, the more I realized that I was writing this book so that I could better understand love and define what it means—not only to my Yellow personality color—but to each of the other colors. You see, I found that this emotion doesn't mean the same thing to each person, nor do we all share the same expectations or express it in the same way. The more I researched the topic, the more I began to understand why loving and being loved can be such a challenge: We don't all see it, give it, or need it in the same way.

Before beginning the writing process, I always ask myself a series of questions, which is an idiosyncrasy of my personality color—always wanting to know and needing to understand. The questions I ask are:

1. Why should this book be written?

2. What value will it be to those who read it?

3. What information can be offered that will positively contribute to the quality of other people's lives?

4. How will this knowledge help people find the love they desire?

5. How will it improve the quality of their relationships?

Yet in preparing for this particular work, my usual list seemed somehow less important, because it was overridden by two more important questions—ones that kept popping up repeatedly as I listened to people talk about love:

1. Why is it that the one thing we need, desire, yearn for, and crave more than anything else is so laden with struggles?

2. Why is it so difficult to sustain a relationship where the needs of both people can be fulfilled?

As I pondered these questions, I realized that the answers could be found in two significant and identifiable elements: personality and its differences. Then I understood why I was writing this book.

The Science of Personality

The research in these pages is primarily based on the *science of personality* and how it impacts who we are, how we act, what love means to us, how we care for others, and even who we want to be with. As a scholar of personality typology for more than 25 years, I utilized my research as well as the discoveries and teachings of Plato, Hippocrates, and Carl Jung to develop an understanding of the inherent part of human nature that's both predictable and observable: personality.

Throughout the book, I refer frequently to the science of personality neurology and the mental functioning associated with it. My intention is to help create an awareness of how it contributes to the formation of stress and tension, and how it triggers misunderstandings and disagreements that build communication barriers, thus making it difficult for us to get on the same wavelength with those we love. I explain how personality differences are the underlying cause of many of the struggles we experience in our romantic relationships; and I offer suggestions, helpful hints, and ways to deal with those issues. I shed light on how each type of person views and expresses love, and offer insight into what each personality color needs in order to feel cherished.

The material you'll be reading is a compilation of different approaches, both scientific and humanistic, and all are designed to help expand your awareness of personality and its effects on love. The different methods include what are considered the hard sciences: personality neurology, neurobiology, neuropsychology, psychoneuroimmunology, and endocrinology. This also takes into consideration the latest research on the differences between the female and the male brain. Then there are what are considered the soft sciences, which include psychology, psychotherapy, and sociology.

The humanistic approach—probably the easiest for us to relate to and the most fun—involves anecdotes offered by the many people who shared their stories, openly discussing their struggles and recounting what they've done to keep their love alive and make their relationships work day in, day out. The information they contributed added heart to the book, and from my perspective made it an understandable living classroom. These individuals took what could have been a difficult and contentious topic and turned it into an exciting and inspiring journey.

The Role of Personality

There's a tremendous price that we pay in our hearts and love relationships when we don't understand the important role that personality plays in how we interact and engage with those we care for. After all, it's our inherent traits that create our perceptions and determine what we need in order to love and feel loved. The more we can understand about this inherent part of who we are, the more we'll find that it isn't as malleable as we'd like to believe.

It's true that there's a part of us that's molded by our conditioning and influenced by external factors, and this aspect of our personality (and the habits and comfort zones it creates) can be changed if we deem it important to do so. However, those traits that are responsible for determining how we gather and process information and make decisions aren't changeable—unless we choose to have a lobotomy!

Let me explain: If you rely on your physical senses of sight, hearing, touch, taste, or smell to gather data, and the information you receive must have meaning before you can make a decision, then you'll follow this process throughout your entire life. On the other hand, if you use your intuition and need to feel the *vibes* in order to gather information, making decisions because they feel right, then you'll stick with that pattern. In other words, the personality traits you're born with are the ones you'll get to live with forever.

Now don't feel trapped—keep in mind that we can all learn to expand the perception we have of ourselves and acquire new interpersonal skills. We can even increase our awareness of personality differences, which helps us become whole-brain thinkers, but we can't change the core essence of our neurology. Besides, those characteristics create our natural talents and give us our inherent strengths. The more we learn about the distinctions of personality, however, the easier it will be for us to get the love we need and to give it to others. The ultimate reward is that we can then create mutually satisfying and long-lasting love relationships.

This ties in to some underlying suppositions that determined the structure of this book and the materials presented, which are:

- Personality traits define who we are, how we act, what love means to us, and how we express it.

- These traits are instrumental in creating many of the expectations that we bring into our love relationships.

- Since there are different types, there are different perceptions of love—and consequently different needs for what it takes to feel cared for.

- Personality traits influence who we're most and least attracted to.

- As there are different meanings of love, there are different kinds of relationships.

The premise of this book is to establish a new way to view our relationships and mates so we can realize that when conflict rears its head, our partner isn't deliberately trying to make our life as miserable as we may think or feel. It's just that they may be a different personality type and consequently see situations differently. I hope that what you'll learn from this book will help you become more tolerant and patient with each other's idiosyncrasies and quirks, and maybe even more compassionate toward yourself.

Who knows? Perhaps we can establish a new way of viewing affection, and maybe even create a new discipline called the "psychonality of love," meaning the science that enables us to understand this force from the perspective of personality.

How Will You Identify Your Personality Color?

I've included an assessment that will enable you to identify your personality color, and in the process help you recognize the color of those you love: your mate, children, siblings, parents, grandparents, aunts, uncles, and oh, yes—friends. There's a general description of each of the personality colors, as well as an in-depth look at what love means to each of them and how they express its splendors: romance, passion, intimacy, sex, communication, and commitment. You'll also find a list of the ten most observable behavioral patterns for each of the colors and an overview of the qualities that make each one unique. And just to make it fun and interesting, there are anecdotes to help you better understand the four personality colors.

Heightened Sensitivity

Any evaluation process that uses names, letters, behavioral-pattern descriptions, and even colors to explain personality types and their differences runs the risk of making people feel boxed in. I've tried to be sensitive to that fact, and I ask that you do the same, using this information with integrity and sensitivity. Here are some helpful suggestions:

- First and foremost, don't use your understanding of personality to discriminate against someone who's different from you. Prejudices of any kind are destructive both to others and to yourself.

- Apply what you've learned to enhance the quality of your love relationships and increase your tolerance.

- Rather than focusing on the negative aspects of your differences, look for similarities and find ways that you complement each other.

- When conflicts arise, don't immediately assume that your mate is out to get you or make your life difficult.

- Use this data as a means of discussing variations in your personal styles. This helps deal with various issues and prevent personal attacks.

- Avoid falling back on your personality color as a means of defending behavior that's hurtful or harmful or using it to make excuses for your actions.

In addition to personality traits, there are other factors that make us individuals that shouldn't be overlooked. There are the differences between males and females, the variations created by ethnic and cultural influences, and those stemming from sexual preferences. As you read this book, be mindful of the unique qualities that each person offers and the fact that it's not my intention to take that away.

I've tried to isolate gender differences as they pertain to the general understanding of personality typology and to eliminate the stereotypical behavior associated with traditional roles. However, when it was important to address something specific as associated with either a male or female personality color, I've identified whether it pertains to a gender. Please keep in mind that my intention is to focus on the predictable and observable behavioral patterns associated with the inherent traits of personality, and not on gender differences.

Another factor I've taken into consideration is the impact that age has on the expression of love, meaning that how a 20-year-old does so will be different from a 40- or 50-year-old. When we look at personality through its inherent neurology, we'll see that in reality, there's no difference other than perhaps the impact of hormones. In the descriptions of each of the colors, there's a section that addresses how the *perception* of love changes with age. What we'll learn is that all personality colors begin to appreciate their different aspects as they get older—their strengths and their weaknesses—and come to understand the richness that both have added to the quality of their lives. We'll discover how it's the appreciation and acceptance of ourselves that is indeed one of the rewards of maturity.

Finally, remember when reading about each of the personality colors that there are no absolutes. We're all a reflection of societal stereotyping and conditioning, so the descriptions are intended to provide a general overview of the behavior that's predictable and observable. They aren't meant to be restrictive or limiting, but rather liberating and empowering. They can be a point of reference and offer a nonthreatening way to discuss differences and provide insight into yourself and those you interact with.

A Changing World

Our world is changing, and so is the perception of what constitutes a love relationship. When evaluating the dynamics of personality and love, the information provided applies to all connections, regardless of sexual preference. It's not focused on anyone specifically, nor is it about gender roles. Consequently, you'll find me using the words *partner* and *mate* interchangeably, versus stereotypical gender words such as *spouse, husband,* or *wife.* The bottom line isn't sexual preference; it's acceptance—of one another, our partner's needs as well as our own, and the contributions that both bring to the relationship—especially when they're different. Having a partner who's supportive, caring, and sensitive, and who encourages personal growth and self-love is far more valuable than someone who seeks to turn us into someone else or tries to mold us into a "mini-them." And besides, love knows no gender differences; it only knows true caring.

The Structure of the Book

Love . . . What's Personality Got to Do with It? is divided into three parts. The first section looks at the nature of love and its many splendors: romance, passion, intimacy, sex, communication, and commitment. It introduces the concept of personality and begins the exploration of how it affects what love means to us, how we care for others, who we cherish, and how we express this.

Part II, "The Four Fabulous Personalities . . . Performing True to Their Colors," is where you'll find the assessment that will help you identify your own personality color. There are comprehensive descriptions of each of the four colors and insights into how each one defines love, expresses its splendors, and the kinds of expectations that each color brings into their relationships. Basically, this is the part of the book where we get down to the nitty-gritty of personality. At the end of each chapter, you'll find tips and helpful hints that can assist you in keeping wonder alive and burning brightly in your relationship.

Part III, "Working at Love to Make Love Work," is where the rubber meets the road because it offers tangible, immediately applicable, and tried-and-true techniques that can be used when personality differences prevent you and your mate from seeing eye to eye. This section identifies the conflict issues common to all relationships and looks at the most complex part of being with someone: communication. There are also dos and don'ts that can help you and your mate avoid falling into those traps and keep the lines of communication open, when the tendency is to clam up and suppress the hurt feelings.

The Afterword ends the book by looking at the importance of self-love and how the lack of it not only affects our ability to give and receive love, but also has an impact on health. You'll learn how this trait is the catalyst for human transformation, and how its energetic vibration helps heal the body, mind, and soul.

A Final Look at Who We Are

It's not my intention to offend any of the personality colors. However, the information I share may do so, especially for those whose emotional nature is to take things personally. I've decided that rather than writing a book that's specifically created to win friends, I prefer to influence people's lives and hopefully enhance the quality of their relationships. The information is offered in a way that sheds light on both the positive and negative qualities of each of the four personality colors, and portrays the real issues that we all must deal with in our interactions with those we love.

As a Yellow, I've set high standards for this work and what it offers you. The fundamental requirement is that you find it informative and useful, not just fluff and hype that looks good on paper but in reality isn't specifically applicable to your relationship or interactions with other people. I hope that what you'll learn from this book will help you either find the love you're looking for or keep what you have. And most of all, I hope that it helps you realize that not everyone sees or expresses this emotion the same way—and that just because it's viewed differently doesn't mean that a relationship can't work. It simply means that you and your mate may have to become more creative and understanding.

In the fast-paced world in which we live, it's easy for us to become too busy or tired to make the effort it takes to keep love alive. We're all seeking ways to help our affection grow and flourish, while at the same time giving both our mate and ourselves what we need in order to feel cherished.

We're all searching and adapting to some extent as we perceive less caring in the world. We're looking passionately for ways to re-create the compassion that can help us learn how to coexist in a world that admonishes differences and seeks to create rigidly patterned behavior. I believe that the key to finding what we're seeking lies in understanding love through the eyes of personality. I hope that this book gives you that key, so you can reach deeply into the reservoir that you hold inside and open your heart to all of the happiness and joy that love offers.

Good luck and good love,
Carol

PART I

Love

CHAPTER ONE

The Nature of Love

Ah, love! The very word stirs within us that deepest, most elusive, and most misunderstood of all human emotions. Its presence puts a bounce in our step and ignites a flame in our hearts that drives us to want and need more of it. It makes us feel happy, whole, satisfied, safe, and secure, and offers us the opportunity to learn more about who we really are.

When we're in love, the perception we have of ourselves expands. We no longer see ourselves as being separate from others, but rather connected to them. Our tolerance for the differences in people increases. We feel empowered to take risks and to move beyond our self-perceived limitations. Our self-confidence is enhanced, so the challenges that life places before us seem less daunting and burdensome, because we know that we don't have to face them alone. It's as if love magically transforms the world into a place that's exciting, exhilarating, and pleasurable.

Love is the reward that comes when we reach out to others and care about them. Its presence is what makes our hearts sing and frees our soul to express itself. This energy makes it possible for us to experience one of the true joys in life and discover what's really important. It changes how we see things and opens our eyes so that we're able to savor the beauty that surrounds us and lies within us. Love encourages us to lighten up and reminds us not to take life or ourselves too seriously. It increases our sensitivity and heightens our awareness in a way that makes it possible for us to recognize the tantalizing subtleties of each day, offer opportunities to find self-love, and reconnect with our inner child. This is the part of each of us that never becomes emotionally wounded, cynical, or fed up with life; the child within us is playful, seeks to experience all that life offers, wants to have fun, and remembers that laughter is the best medicine.

Yet even knowing all that love offers, we tend to make demands of it and burden it with unrealistic expectations. We expect it to save us from our loneliness, protect us from painful situations, and make us happy. We want it to magically transmute our inadequacies and manifest that special someone who'll shelter us from the trials and tribulations of life, creating a caring and nurturing environment where we can just be ourselves. We expect love to be a fix-all, do-all, and cure-all. Unfortunately, those who approach love in this way find that it will seldom fulfill their fantasies, nor will they come to know its true nature or understand how it can add richness to the quality of their lives.

But why wouldn't we want to experience all that love offers? Why do we make choices that limit it and that cause us to not trust it? And even more important, why do we leave learning about love and what it takes to develop a strong relationship to the observation of our parents or other people? Wouldn't you think that finding out more about something that impacts our lives so dramatically would have been a mandatory part of preparing for life? Just imagine how much heartache could have been spared, how many emotional hurts could have been avoided, and how many hours of mental anguish could have been eliminated if we'd just been taught that the nature of love is:

1. Accepting. Love teaches us to not only accept others for who *they* are but to do the same for ourselves and who *we* are. Through acceptance, we can grow, flourish, and weather the stormy times that are an inherent part of any relationship. This quality creates a safe place where we can meet heart to heart, mind to mind, and body to body without the fear of being vulnerable or having our weaknesses used against us. This makes it possible to take risks both on our own and as a couple and supports individuality and independence.

2. Unconditional. Love isn't meant to be manipulative or hurtful, but is supposed to create an environment where we can feel safe expressing our emotional needs and wants. When love is offered unconditionally, it fosters the kind of sacred union where passion, caring, generosity, and kindness drive how we interact with each other. This quality supports creating a collaborative relationship where both people can realize their full potential, and where there's a level of openheartedness and emotional honesty.

3. Forgiving. Love requires being able to say "I'm sorry," both to those we've hurt and to ourselves. The inability to forgive is like taking poison and waiting for our spirit to die. On the other hand, letting go removes the emotional charges we have around our hurts and frees our heart so that we can transform the limitations and expectations those injuries have created. Forgiveness is to see others and ourselves through the eyes of compassion, and it offers the opportunity for personal growth.

4. Nonjudgmental. Love becomes safe when there's no judgment and the fear of criticism is removed. This means accepting each other's personality idiosyncrasies and quirks and not finding fault with who the other person is. It conveys the message that we're glad that our mate is in our life and shows that we appreciate what they bring to the relationship. Most important, it minimizes the potential for conflict.

5. Respectful. Love deepens when there's respect. Its presence in a relationship expresses admiration and tells our mate that we trust their judgment and have a high regard for their intelligence. It's what makes our relationship sweeter, more passionate, and more meaningful, and it opens the door to the kind of intimacy that promotes the sharing of our deepest emotional needs. One of the greatest gifts we can give our mate is respect, and it's one of the greatest cultivators of a mutually satisfying relationship.

6. Collaborative. Love involves an equal amount of give-and-take, and requires the ability to set aside the needs of the individual to nurture the couple. In relationships where being a couple is the objective, both people look for ways to work together and to complement each other, thus enhancing each other's strengths and minimizing weaknesses. Being collaborative means that both people give 100 percent of themselves and treat each other as they want to be treated.

7. Expressive. Love supports the expression of thoughts, emotions, concerns, fears, and vulnerabilities. Being able to talk about what is on our minds and how we're feeling makes us feel good about our relationship and deepens the emotional connection we have with our mate. Love thrives when the lines of communication are kept open, and it withers and dies when they break down. Feeling silenced is a great destroyer of intimacy.

8. Abundant. Love adds a richness and wealth to life that money can't buy. Its energy exudes a contagious happiness, and like a magnet attracts more joy to us. In order for love to be abundant, we must express our appreciation for all that we have and feel, and through words of gratitude tell our mate, "Thank you for being in my life," "Thank you for loving me," and "Thank you for making my life so rich."

9. Openhearted. Love takes courage and an open heart. It requires trust and the willingness to follow our heart rather than listen to our head. This is the foundation upon which we build our closest and most intimate relationships, and it allows us to meet our mate on common ground. When we see our partner through our heart, we're able to see an inner beauty that may not be visible to the eyes.

10. Separate and together. Love encourages individuality and supports autonomy—its nature is to include both separateness and togetherness. Couples who feel secure in themselves and in their relationship have the freedom to spend time with their friends, cultivate their own interests, be themselves, and explore the potential they hold inside. Those who believe that in order to show their love they must always be together foster an unhealthy codependency on each other, create feelings of isolation, stifle individuality, and many times end up with strong feelings of resentment. If a relationship is to remain healthy, both aspects are essential.

11. Evolutionary. Love is constantly changing and moving through different stages as it grows and evolves. Each phase— meeting, dating, courtship, engagement, commitment, and growing together as a couple—offers a multitude of opportunities, all of which are intended to help us learn more about ourselves and those we care for. Love, like all of life, has its cycles and seasons. It's an ongoing journey that requires that both people stay actively involved in its evolutionary process and focus on moving it in the same direction—the one that fulfills each other's deepest emotional needs.

Love Isn't Brain Surgery

It's true that on the surface love appears to be complicated, challenging, and sometimes even frightening. However, by understanding its nature, we can see that it isn't all that mysterious, nor is creating a loving relationship as complex as brain surgery. This state really asks very little from us other than that we approach it with an open heart and live it without expectations. In return, it gives us the chance to experience all of its many splendors and to savor one of life's greatest pleasures. It creates a safe, secure place where we can feel supported as we move through our own personal growth stages by letting us see ourselves through the eyes of those who care for us. If we could remember that the intention of love is to enhance the quality of our lives, then removing the expectations we have around it is neither scary nor difficult.

A Final Thought to Ponder

You can never really change anyone. The best you can do is offer them love.

CHAPTER TWO

The Splendors of Love

Have you ever paid attention to how much we get bombard-ed, both subtly and not so subtly, with messages about love? There are those intended to create the image of what perfect love should look like, those that tell us how to find or keep love rela-tionships, and those that tell us how we should *act* when we're in love. Love messages appear to be everywhere—on television and radio, in magazines and advertising, in conversations, on the Internet, and of course, there are endless books on the subject. We seem to be obsessed in our search to find true love, to capture its essence, understand it, and master it once we connect with it. Is our inherent primordial longing so strong that we'll virtually de-vour any book or buy any product that holds within it the promise of finding everlasting love? The answer is yes!

Yet as we voraciously read these books, trying out their sug-gestions and buying the products intended to turn us into love attractors, we still seem to find ourselves feeling unfulfilled and unsatisfied, not knowing how to partake in the wonders that love offers. But what are love's many splendors? They're all the differ-ent means we use to say "I love you," "I care about you," and "I want to spend my life with you." They're the words and actions that tell our mates how happy we are that they're in our lives. They sustain a relationship when the initial excitement of falling in love wears off, and they make us more receptive to hanging in there when trying to work through our differences. These splendors of love are romance, passion, intimacy, sex, communication, and commitment.

Romance . . . the Icing on the Cake

Romance titillates the mind and stimulates our imagination. It's what adds the zip and gusto to our interactions and brings the element of excitement into loving and being loved. It entices us into wanting to participate in a love relationship and is primarily responsible for sparking the flames of passion that create an environment where we can explore the pleasures of each other's company. This quality promotes open and honest communication, strengthens commitment, and expresses to those we love that they hold a special place in our heart.

Romantic gestures make it possible for us to eloquently express how we feel without having to necessarily utter the words. They create a safe haven where we can share our deepest needs, verbalize our concerns, reveal our fears, and let our differences come forth in a playful, lighthearted way. Some of the more common expressions of romance include:

- Dinner at a favorite restaurant
- Snuggling in front of a fire
- Holding hands
- A gentle touch when it isn't expected
- A wink, smile, or hug
- Placing a rose on a pillow
- Sending a card that simply says
  "Just thinking about you" or "I love you"
- A bouquet of flowers
- A box of candy
- A surprise weekend getaway to a special place

When it comes to being romantic, the only limitation is our imagination.

Passion . . . the Irresistible Desire to Be Loved

Passion is the strong emotion generated by romance. It's the element of our humanity that isn't governed by the mind or reasoning, but is driven by the needs of the heart and the desires of the body. This is the unadulterated expression of love, and its job is to send the seductive, sensual signals that better things are to follow. When this fire arouses us, it conveys the message that we're turned on, ready to engage physically and sexually, and are excited by the other person and their actions. Passion is intended to intensify our desire for intimacy; it's what we commonly call "the heat of the moment."

The expressions of passion are the tingles we feel when that special someone touches our skin, gives us an intense kiss, strokes our body, and whispers how they feel in our ear. It's the rush of warmth that causes us to feel flushed, that creates butterflies in our stomach, and makes our heart pound so hard that we think it will explode. When this energy stirs, there's no mistaking it—and in most cases, no controlling it. It seems to have a mind of its own, and all we can do is sit back and enjoy it.

Intimacy . . . the Miracle of Love

Intimacy is our soul's way of finding physical expression. It's what adds depth to love and gives it meaning. When exploring each of the splendors of love, we find that this is the most complicated to understand, because we can't always put it into words. It's the part of love that's fragile and the most vulnerable to succumbing to the expectations created by emotional hurts. However, it also offers us the greatest opportunity to learn more about ourselves and those we love, because it teaches compassion and forgiveness. It's intimacy that helps us feel secure in our relationship and comforts us physically, emotionally, mentally, and spiritually. Its presence is imperative if love is to grow and flourish.

This quality manifests in different ways, and the ones we're most inclined to use are those determined by our inherent personality needs. It's for this reason that not everyone defines or shows it in the same way, or has the same needs with respect to it. The expressions are physical, emotional, mental, and spiritual intimacy.

1. Physical Intimacy. This is probably the easiest for us to understand and recognize because it's experienced through our five senses: sight, touch, hearing, taste, and smell. This expression of intimacy uses the sensations of the body to tell us when we're physically stimulated and ready to exchange sexual pleasures with our mate.

2. Emotional Intimacy. As physical intimacy satisfies the needs of the body, emotional intimacy satisfies the needs of the heart. This brings voice to our deepest and innermost emotional needs, connecting us heart to heart. It cultivates the deep caring we feel for our mate and strengthens the bond we have with them. In this way, we send the message that we trust them implicitly with our hearts, feelings, dreams, desires, and love.

3. Mental Intimacy. This quality creates a nonverbal connection that allows us to anticipate the needs of our mate and that helps us understand why they act as they do. Being mentally in sync describes mental intimacy, and it happens when we know our mate so well that we can predict how they'll react or respond in any given situation. This kind of closeness implies being on the same wavelength, to the point that we can finish our mate's sentences and sense what they're thinking.

4. Spiritual Intimacy. In this expression of affection, two hearts become one, and the souls meet to form a sacred union. It's the common ground where love becomes unconditional, and the needs of the couple override those of the individual. This allows us to catch a glimpse of the specialness and uniqueness we hold inside, and makes it possible for us to see ourselves through the eyes of our mate. The bond created by spiritual intimacy can turn an ordinary relationship into an extraordinary one and magically weaves souls together through the profound ties of the heart.

Sex . . . Dessert for the Attitude

Sex is the crowning glory of the human desire to feel loved, and it contributes significantly to our overall sense of well-being. It weaves all the splendors of love together, bringing forth the physical expression of intimacy. This is one of the most elemental pleasures associated with a romantic partner and creates an environment where we can show physical appreciation for one another. Each time we exchange sexual pleasures, we have the opportunity to re-create something new in our relationship, reinforce our commitment to each other, discover more about what gives each other joy, and find all of the special ways to say "I love you" through the sensations of the body.

Sex, as with the other splendors of love, fulfills our basic human needs biologically, emotionally, and mentally. It forms a sacred union between two people, thus making it possible for us to experience all the levels of intimacy. This connection allows us to meet body to body and communicate how we feel without verbalization. It unleashes strong erotic feelings and keeps the heat of passion burning in our heart and in our bodies. Most important, it opens the door to sharing the essence of our being.

Communication . . . the Language of Love

Communication involves both talking and listening. This language gives voice to all the splendors of love and makes it possible for us to share our thoughts and feelings, knowing that someone who cares will listen. The need to connect with each other is as essential as love itself and is the key to experiencing this emotion in a healthy way. When these lines are open, the transfer of information heightens our sensitivity to our mate's needs and sensitizes us to how we interact with them. Open communication deepens the feelings we have and makes the relationship stronger and the bond of commitment more solid—sturdy enough to withstand the misunderstandings and conflict that arise when we don't share the same perspectives. It ensures that we're on the same page in our dreams, desires, and goals.

The kind of love relationship we all hope for is the one where we feel safe in sharing our feelings and can do so without the fear of retribution or being silenced. This can only be achieved when we have the security that comes with a mature, sensitive, intelligent, and intimate commitment. The communication process involves four steps: speaking, listening, responding, and acknowledging. When any of these steps are eliminated, the process becomes stressful and the lines of communication break down. It's this collapse that creates frustration and resentment, makes us feel isolated and undervalued, and generates the hurt feelings that could ultimately cause the relationship to fail. It seems that the greatest problem with communication is the *illusion* that it has been achieved.

Commitment . . . Proof That Love Is Alive

Commitment is proof that love is alive and that the relationship is healthy. It's the foundation upon which long-term partnerships are able to support themselves through all of the highs and lows that occur as they move through different evolutionary stages. It adds the elements of stability, security, safety, predictability, and continuity. When we make a commitment to someone to share our heart, we're sending the message that we trust them and feel a deep emotional connection with them. We're saying, "I care about you," "I want to take care of you," "You can always count on me being there for you," and "I want to spend the rest of my life with you."

The level of commitment we feel around our love relationship is always changing—it's either growing or waning. When it's the former, the connection we feel strengthens, and our willingness to expend the effort to make love work increases. However, if how we feel about our mate diminishes, so does the desire to commit to making it work. A romantic partnership is no different from raising a child. It's a living, breathing, dynamic entity that needs to feel loved, be nurtured and cared for, receive support and direction, and get constant attention if it's going to grow into something that we can be proud of. It needs the commitment that both people are going to be there for each other through both the good and stressful times.

When We're in Love

When we're in love, the world around us looks different, our attitude toward life improves, and how we feel inside changes. The more we understand how the splendors of love add to the quality of a relationship, the easier it becomes for us to create the kind of connection that we need, desire, and deserve. The more we express these qualities, the easier it is to create a mutually satisfying partnership and give our mate what they need in order to feel cherished.

As we use these splendors in our interactions with each other, it's easier to focus on our similarities and overlook our incompatibilities. If we can remember that it's these wonderful attributes that are responsible for keeping love alive and sustaining the feelings we have for our mate, then maybe we'll be less inclined to only wait for those special occasions to say "I love you" or show how we feel. Perhaps expressing them and engaging in them each day will take on a new meaning and a new importance.

These joys and how we express them offer the greatest opportunity to make sense of our need for this emotional connection . . . especially when combined with knowledge of the personality of love.

CHAPTER THREE

The Personality of Love

Welcome to the wonderful world of personality—and *yes,* contrary to what you may sometimes think, everyone does have a personality.

The understanding of this subject offers a tremendous opportunity to not only learn more about who we are, but to better comprehend those we care for. Personality, as with love, is a strong motivator of human behavior and is an integral part of what makes us who we are, because it's the primary organizing principle that determines why we think and act the way we do. These characteristics are responsible for influencing the development and function of the activities of our brain, and for creating the patterns of behavior we display that are both predictable and observable. It's these inherent qualities that find their expression very early on and remain consistent throughout our lives. Our personality defines what love means to us and how we express its splendors.

My Interest in Personality

As long as I can remember, I've been interested in learning more about what makes people tick and what motivates them to do the things they do. I've been intrigued by the fact that while we're all certainly different from each other, there's something unspoken that causes us to resemble some people and not others. I was curious about why those who were similar also shared interests, sought parallel experiences, and had comparable needs and wants. I wanted to know why they used the same words to express their thoughts and feelings, and why they had the same frustrations relating to communication. It was as if I were driven by an insatiable need to find these answers, because on some level I knew that if I did, I'd be able to understand why I always seemed to be marching to a different drummer than the people around me. It was that insatiable need to know that ultimately led me to pursue an education in personality behavioral psychology.

What I discovered about personality not only transformed my life, it changed the perception I had of myself, the way I looked at others, and how I interacted with them. It helped me understand that my persistently analytical nature, my need to solve other people's problems (whether they wanted my help or not), and my hairsplitting disposition was just a natural part of the inherent traits of my personality. It helped me realize that I drove my family, friends, and teachers crazy because I was different than they were, but that there was nothing wrong with them or with me. It opened my eyes to the knowledge that if I was ever going to create a long-term relationship, I'd better be sure that my partner was compatible with my personality and shared the same needs, values, and principles. I recognized that if he didn't, there was a very good chance that the bond wouldn't last.

My understanding of personality not only gave me the answers I was looking for, but it showed me that there are some aspects of human behavior that can be changed and some that can't. It taught me to appreciate those unchangeable parts because that's where we'll find our inner strength, discover our natural talents, and learn to embrace our uniqueness.

What I Learned Along the Way

Typical of my personality, once I set my mind on something, I was tireless in my need to understand the hows and whys of whatever my attention was focused on. Consequently, I've spent more than 25 years studying and researching the effects that personality has on our lives, relationships, and health. I've counseled and interviewed thousands of people in my quest to understand and find answers. What I learned along the way is that regardless of whether it was team-building or management training in the corporate world, or teaching couples how to deal with their differences, it still all boiled down to personality and the need to understand each other.

People wanted to know what they could do to make their relationships work, how they could make them more satisfying, and what they needed to do to be more effective in dealing with their differences. I can't tell you how many times I've been asked, "Is there such a thing as the perfect mate or the perfect relationship?" Everyone wanted to know if there was any hope in finding or creating a love relationship that could give them what they needed, one that could endure the trials and tribulations inherent in sharing their lives together.

I discovered that when people were similar in personality, they defined love the same way, shared the same desires and needs, and used the same criteria to determine what they required in order to feel cherished and accepted. I learned that because of their similarities, they were more successful in creating mutually satisfying long-term relationships. I also found that while opposites attract in the initial stages of putting a relationship together, their differences quickly turned to irritation once the excitement and newness wore off—and ultimately became the primary source of their problems.

Those who were opposites complained of being tired and disenchanted with love, questioning why they were still together. I found that in these situations, there was more energy being put into attempting to change or control each other than trying to find ways to make things work. As I interviewed couples with personality differences, I discovered that the general belief was that the relationship was frustrating, a struggle, and emotionally unsatisfying.

Another bit of insight I gained in the course of my research was that many people placed a greater value on the ability to communicate than they did on any of the other splendors of love. Many told me candidly that the greatest source of frustration in their relationship was the inability to talk to each other and share their feelings. The consensus was that communication problems are the primary reason for many failed partnerships because they're the most difficult to resolve and overcome, and are where there's the least willingness to change or accept personality differences.

Seeing Those You Love from the Perspective of Personality

If we were to look at each other purely from the outer appearances of how we go through the normal activities of daily life, we'd find that there's really not much difference between those we love and ourselves. Basically, we're all trying to survive, and we continually look for ways to see that our human needs are met. We all work to move ahead personally and try to do our best to get through each day with as few problems, traumas, and conflicts as we can. Yet if we were to look beyond those superficial appearances and examine the more subtle aspects (such as communication quirks, coping mechanisms, decision-making styles, and the other things that affect whether we feel loved and accepted), we'd quickly discover that most of us aren't the same at all. In order for love to grow, flourish, and sustain itself, we must understand its subtleties, because these can add to the quality of our relationships or potentially undermine them to the point where the lines of communication break down.

An added benefit to seeing those we love from the perspective of personality is that it heightens our sensitivity to the nonverbal communication patterns others use to let us know how they're feeling. These practices tell us if they're happy, unhappy, stressed, distressed, or burdened. We can get this information from their demeanor, posture, voluntary gestures (such as facial grimaces and frowning), and involuntary gestures (such as holding their breath, sweating, or turning red in the face when angry). The more we learn about personality, the more we come to understand how it acts as a sophisticated communication system that's constantly transmitting messages, telling each other what we need, want, and desire. It alerts us when adjustments need to be made and tells us what kinds of changes are necessary if we are to keep the lines of communication open.

Are We Born This Way?

One of the most frequently asked questions I hear when talking about personality is, "Are we born this way?" The answer is *yes*. Personality, for the most part, is inherent. In other words, it's in your genes. To help explain my response, I ask people to answer the following questions:

- Have you ever noticed that you seem to be attracted to some people and not to others?

- Are you aware that you'll consistently tend to respond and react to specific situations and to certain people in the same way over and over again?

- Have you noticed that there are certain tasks you just don't like to do, and subsequently, will procrastinate in doing them or will find ways to avoid them completely?

- Do you make your decisions based on what feels right to you, or based on logic and what makes sense?

Then I tell these people that how they answered these questions is determined by the part of their personality they were born with.

I explain how this inherent part of us operates in much the same way that automatic pilot does, always guiding us to our desired destination, while ensuring that we don't get off course in the process (meaning we don't make wrong decisions). If our personality perceives that we're about to make a decision that isn't in our best interests, it will mentally or emotionally sound the alarm by creating confusion or stress. These sirens are intended to alert us that a course correction is needed immediately because the direction we're headed isn't where we want to go. They're telling us that there's a good chance the decision we're about to make is going to compromise some aspect of our personality, or worse yet, cause us to engage in self-sabotaging behavior.

It's the responsibility of our personality to see that we function within our inherent strengths rather than from our weaknesses. It understands that when we're forced to work from our weaknesses, we tend to feel bad about ourselves and create false perceptions related to what we're capable of achieving. The inherent part of who we are holds within it our natural talents and helps us utilize our innate abilities. It represents our genetic neurological coding, which tells our brain how it should gather and process information and make decisions. This creates both predictable and observable behavior.

Personality is the organizing principle that oversees how we live our lives. It drives how we interact with people, determines the kinds of tasks we enjoy and which ones we don't, defines what love means to us, influences how we express affection, and is primarily responsible for creating the majority of expectations that we bring into our relationships. Through our personality, we express our thoughts, beliefs, attitudes, perceptions, values, hopes, fears, emotions, strengths, and weaknesses. It's what establishes our boundaries and ultimately influences the direction our lives will take.

When the experiences of life complement the boundaries established by our personality type, we function within our strengths, feel good about ourselves, and are able to expand the perceptions we have of what we're capable of achieving. We enjoy an overall sense of well-being and feel more confident. Our interactions with people are less stressful because we're open to what they have to offer. We're able to communicate our needs more effectively and in a straightforward manner.

On the other hand, when we find ourselves in situations and relationships that aren't in alignment with the boundaries set by our personality, we become stressed, confused, and emotionally agitated. Our mind begins to focus on our fears, inadequacies, and weaknesses, and we feel energetically drained. We become restless, distressed, and unhappy with ourselves, engaging in negative self-talk and becoming overly critical and judgmental of ourselves. It's in these times that our personality steps in and sounds the alarm, telling us that it's time to either remove ourselves from the situation or relationship or make some much-needed changes in our lives.

What Creates Our Personality Type?

By now you're probably getting a pretty good idea of just how important your personality is in determining who you truly are, and are beginning to understand how much it impacts all the things you do. However, before we move on to the next part of the book, where you'll have the opportunity to identify your personality color, let's take a closer look at what we mean by *personality type*. This term describes all the aspects of the personality that contribute to making us who we are and that create our uniqueness. Those parts are traits and characteristics, and their combination forms the identity we project to the outer world and determines how we express it. Differentiating between these two components can be tricky when trying to make sense of someone's behavior. However, you just have to keep in mind that *traits* are inherent and create predictable behavior, and *characteristics* represent learned behavior and are responsible for creating habits and comfort zones.

Traits

Traits direct the mental activities of the brain, meaning that they tell it how to gather and process data and make decisions. They act as both filters and initiators of information. As filters, traits sort through and evaluate input to see if it matches our past experiences. They're continually checking, cross-checking, and monitoring the quality of the information collected to ensure that it's pertinent, reliable, and viable, and determining if it's of value to our decision-making process. Traits are only interested in what's relevant to how we think and feel. They also help us cut through the smoke screens created by characteristics, thus enabling our mind to differentiate between what our own needs are versus those of others. Traits help us get to the core of our issues and enable us to understand our experiences so that we can find both meaning and purpose in them.

As the initiators of thoughts and feelings, traits serve as course correctors when we stray outside the boundaries they've established. They heighten mental and emotional awareness so that we can recognize when we aren't making decisions in alignment with our mental functioning. Their prime concern is that we don't fall into the mental limitations created by characteristics or create behavior that's counterproductive to the life and relationships we desire and deserve. They help us avoid situations, experiences, and relationships that may cause distorted perceptions of who we are and what we're capable of.

In the communication process, traits play an important role because they determine the words we use to express how we feel and convey what we're thinking. For example, some personality types will use the word *think* to describe what's going on in their head, and others will use the word *feel* to describe what's in their heart. The people who make decisions based on logic, on what makes sense, and who are analytical in nature, will tell you what they *think* and why they're *thinking* that. On the other hand, those who make decisions because they *feel* right will tell you how they *feel* and why they *feel* the decision is either a good or bad one.

Now, applying this information to the communication process, if a *feeling* personality type asks a *thinking* personality type how they *feel* about something, the *thinking* personality type isn't going to know how to respond because the word *feeling* isn't a part of their decision-making criteria. As a rule, the *thinking* personality won't respond because they can't relate to what's being asked. Unfortunately, the lack of response sends an emotionally charged message to the *feeling* personality that the *thinking* personality isn't interested in what they have to say or in what they're *feeling*. Consequently, their *feelings* are hurt, and the lines of communication quickly deteriorate and break down. However, if the *feeling* personality asked the *thinking* personality what they *think,* then the conversation would flow smoothly and both would get what they need. Wow! It's no wonder we have trouble understanding each other or getting on the same wavelength.

Characteristics

Characteristics represent learned behavior, reflect our conditioning, and create patterns intended to help us fit into our social structure and keep us compliant. When it comes to understanding personality type, it's probably easier for us to recognize the influence of characteristics than traits. This is because characteristics create the habits, comfort zones, and behavior that cause us to avoid risks, not want to change, and not be open to trying new things. They reflect our conditioning and how other people see us or want us to be, but don't represent who we really are. They basically mirror our biographical history, and for the most part, they're the reason we find ourselves repeating the same experiences, dealing with the same problems, and creating the same kinds of dysfunctional relationships over and over again.

Characteristics are insidious and can be difficult to change because of the strong hold they have on our behavior and thinking. They feed our fears and support staying where we are because it's safe and comfortable. A good example of this is when we find ourselves remaining in a dysfunctional relationship even when our mind and heart are telling us to get out of it. Characteristics promote taking a wait-and-see approach and encourage handing over the control of our lives to someone else because we believe that they're a better judge of what we need or what we're capable of.

It should be noted that many of the fears we deal with on an ongoing basis result from learned behavior and conditioning. We aren't born with fears, nor are they created by our traits. They come from other people's fears, insecurities, and perceptions of us. Unfortunately, most of the fears we struggle with as adults were imprinted in the early years of our lives. Perhaps the reasons we rely so heavily on our characteristics is because we know that they'll give us what we need—they create the behavior that helps us fit in and feel accepted. However, the real issue is that they aren't always in alignment with our traits, and consequently create unnatural behavior. Characteristics encourage conformity rather than individuality.

What I Hope You've Learned Along the Way

As you come to know yourself better and understand the significant role that traits play in molding who we are and what we become, I hope you'll begin to see yourself in a new light and view others through a different lens. I hope that how you interact with people will change, and rather than relying on first impressions, you'll become a keen observer of the qualities associated with personality traits. The more you learn, the more you'll recognize how every interaction with someone is a learning experience and presents the opportunity to get rid of some of the characteristics that could potentially be holding you back. This knowledge can teach you how to cope with and tolerate people who are different from you, and help you see that when they challenge you and become confrontational, they aren't necessarily trying to make your life miserable. They just see things in another way.

Perhaps you'll even begin to understand that coming from the same environment doesn't mean that all of your family members will share the same personality type. This bit of insight alone can help you understand why families experience the interesting dynamics they do, and why we don't always see eye to eye. And I hope you've learned that if you're willing to expand the perception you have of yourself beyond the limitations of your characteristics, you'll see how the traits you chose are the ones best suited to help you learn more about life, grow personally, and assist you in your spiritual evolution. You might even see how they can help you fulfill your soul's purpose.

A Final Thought to Ponder

There are many paths we can take to find out who we really are. The most expedient route is the one that comes from understanding our personality type. The slowest relies on other people to tell us who we are and what we're capable of.

PART II

The Four Fabulous Personalities ... Performing True to Their Colors

CHAPTER FOUR

What's Your Personality Color?

Okay, now on to the really exciting stuff: discovering what your personality color is, learning more about who you really are and why you do the things you do, and finding out more about those you love from the perspective of personality. However, before we begin, I feel that I must offer this warning: Once you step into the world of personality and find out all it has to offer, the way you see yourself and other people will change forever. You'll no longer be able to people-watch without finding yourself wondering what everyone's personality color is. You may even find yourself compelled to share what you know with anyone who's open to listening—even total strangers. And if you're single, don't be surprised if you find yourself using your understanding to help you find just who Mr. or Ms. Right will be for you. In any case, how you view human behavior is about to change.

Let's start by first establishing some guidelines to keep in mind as you move forward:

— All personality colors are equally valuable, and each contributes positively to our lives in what they bring into a relationship. There's no personality of choice, and none is better or worse than any of the others. All have their individual strengths and weaknesses (the strengths of one color are usually the weaknesses of another).

— We're all unique, and although the understanding of personality offers insight into people's traits, this isn't an exact science. There are many variables that contribute to making us who we are, such as external influences and a myriad of characteristics created by our conditioning. Just because you may be the same personality color as someone else doesn't mean that they'll be a clone of you, or you of them. What you share are similarities in your neurological hardwiring and behavioral patterns associated with traits.

— If you're in a relationship with someone who isn't your personality color, don't immediately assume it won't work, and definitely don't throw in the towel! Being different doesn't mean that your relationship is doomed. It just means that you may both have to put in more effort to keep the lines of communication open. Remember, compatibility begins with you.

Personality Through the Identity of Color

Ever since I first started working with personality and evaluating the ways to identify different kinds of people, I found myself somewhat confused and unable to remember after 30 days what *my* personality type was. You see, I couldn't relate to the terms that were used to describe the differences. Some assessments used letters to designate personality, others used numbers, and still others used word labels that were offensive, limiting, or too vague. I thought, *If I'm having this kind of trouble and it's my expertise, what's happening to other people? Are they having the same problem?* What I learned became the catalyst for creating the Personality Color Indicator (PCI) that you'll soon be using to identify yourself.

In my quest to find a better way to describe our nature, I came across the work of Dr. Max Lüscher, who used color to explain different personality types. He believed that color had both an emotional and physiological value, and that a person's reaction to specific hues revealed their inherent personality traits. His research provided conclusive evidence that certain shades created the same psychological, emotional, and physiological reactions in people who shared similar personalities. While acknowledging that the measurement of emotions was not completely possible, Dr. Lüscher based the reliability and viability of his work on the measurement of psychological and physiological reactions. As a result of his findings, he developed a test that used color to identify the four different types of personalities.

Color: A Common Language

Integrating Dr. Lüscher's work with my own research and then adding my knowledge to the psychology of color, I began to recognize that color is a common language we all use to describe how we're feeling and where we are emotionally. I discovered that some personality types' behavior matched the responses to specific shades, and indeed, as Dr. Lüscher had found, color could be used to describe personality traits. An added benefit that came from using this technique to describe personality behavior is that the discomfort people felt around being labeled went away. I found that the language of color was a nonthreatening way to talk about differences and made it possible for individuals to express their feelings and uniqueness without resorting to labeling. And most important, I found that months and even years after taking the PCI assessment, people could still remember their personality color.

While my work certainly parallels that of Dr. Lüscher, and we're both in agreement that color is a valuable way to look at personality type, this is not to imply that anyone is trapped in just one color. Sometimes situations and circumstances require that we step outside our traits and learn how to interact as a rainbow. I found that using color as the basis for understanding personality allows us to function as different colors without feeling compromised or stressed. However, we can only do so for a short period—not for a lifetime.

Each day we use color to talk about what we see or how we're feeling. We describe feeling down as being blue; we're red with anger, green with envy, or just plain yellow (meaning that we lack the courage to face an issue that needs attention). We talk about the clear blue sky, yellow sunbeams, green forests, and golden fields of wheat. No matter what the gender, age, conditioning, external influences or personality traits, this is language we can all relate to and seem to be comfortable using as a means of expression.

Color also has a powerful impact on our moods and the physiology of our body. It literally affects us both internally and externally and can change how we feel emotionally. Different hues can increase or decrease our heart rate, change our breathing, stimulate or suppress our desire to eat, and even impact our level of concentration. The vitality we get from color helps us cope with the challenges of life, while at the same time gives us the energy we need to get through our daily activities. It can relax us and can be used to promote healing.

What Color Is Your Personality?

Each of us holds an untapped potential inside that's just waiting for the right opportunity to express itself. One way to turn that potential into reality is to deepen your understanding of who you are and why you do the things you do. Identifying your personality color is the first step in the exciting self-discovery process. By knowing your color, you'll start to see yourself differently, and you'll also begin to understand why some relationships worked and others didn't. There's a very good chance that how you see those you love will change, and you may even find yourself being able to identify their personality colors. No matter how you choose to use this knowledge, you'll find that your life will be rich with color. It will be as though you're looking through the lens of a kaleidoscope: lots of beautiful colors interacting differently with each other, and always becoming more beautiful than before.

The Personality Color Indicator you're about to take is a self-reflective assessment, meaning that you don't need a psychological professional to administer it, score it, or interpret its findings. The PCI is self-scoring and very user-friendly. It consists of 60 statements, each of which is designed to talk to specific parts of your brain with the intention of revealing your personality traits. You'll choose the sentences that apply to you, and the self-scoring aspect of the assessment will help you identify your highest score. Once this score is determined, it will be associated with one of four different colors: *red, orange, yellow,* or *green*.

I urge you—and your mate, if you're in a relationship—to complete the assessment before moving on to the next chapters. I suggest that the two of you take the assessment together because what you'll learn can immediately be put to good use. You'll suddenly have a communication vehicle to talk about your similarities and discuss your differences in a nonthreatening way. You'll find the words needed to express your appreciation for what each of you brings to the relationship. Besides, taking it together can be a lot of fun.

The best approach for making your selections is to determine whether you think or feel that the statement best describes you overall. Respond to each statement based on your first instinctive reaction and how you initially feel about it. Don't get bogged down wondering whether you act one way at work and another way at home. Be as honest with yourself as you can—this isn't about winning a popularity contest.

There's also no point in trying to deceive yourself or be someone other than who you really are. And, for all of you analytical and logical personality types, don't spend a lot of time trying to psych out the assessment or manipulate its outcome. All this will do is cause confusion and wind your mind up to the point that it can't make a decision. One final reminder: There aren't any right or wrong choices, nor can you pass or fail.

Instructions

1. Read each statement carefully, and if that sentence describes you and you agree with it, circle the letter to the left of it. It helps if you respond from the earliest recollections of how you were as a child, and not from the perspective of who you've become.

2. If you don't relate to a statement, skip it and move on to the next one. You don't have to mark every one. In fact, if the sentence and the words in it aren't something you can relate to, you'll naturally be hesitant about circling the letter. When this occurs, it will be your traits talking. Don't circle the letter for that statement.

3. Some personalities will consciously try to beat the test, while another personality type will try to look for patterns in order to skew the results. After 20 years of fine-tuning the PCI, I'll just say up front that because these statements talk to your brain, it's difficult to manipulate the results. I've even seen people who've taken it ten times or more with the thought of intentionally trying to change the final outcome find out that their personality color remains the same. In fact, what they usually discover is that their numbers get stronger in their personality color each time they take it. It seems that the more we learn about who we are, the less willing we are to become someone else.

Once you finish the assessment, follow the self-scoring directions. They'll help you determine your personality color.

The Personality Color Indicator

A   1. I consider myself to be down-to-earth.

A   2. I prefer to stick to a set daily routine rather than put myself in unfamiliar situations.

B 3. I enjoy using my creativity to come up with innova-
       tive ways of doing things rather than doing them the
       way that everyone else does.

A 4. I stay focused, and concentrate on what needs to be
       completed now rather than thinking about future
       tasks.

B 5. I become bored with tasks that are repetitious and
       find myself looking for different and better methods
       of doing them.

B 6. I enjoy the challenge of finding solutions to prob-
       lems that are complex and that need to be explored
       from a variety of perspectives.

A 7. I consider myself to be practical, not theoretical.

B 8. I have a lot of thoughts in my head simultaneously,
       and I'm often accused of not listening or of being
       preoccupied.

A 9. I'd rather work with facts and figures than theories
       and ideas.

B 10. I pride myself on using my intellect and being a
       creative problem solver.

A 11. I'd rather deal with the known than explore possi-
       bilities.

B 12. I prefer being original rather than traditional.

B 13. I'm interested in how machines and products work
       so I can come up with ways to improve them.

B 14. I prefer learning new skills more than using old ones.

A 15. I'm detail oriented.

A 16. I find myself attracted to people who are similar to me: realistic, practical, and involved with current issues.

A 17. I become impatient and frustrated with problems or tasks that are too complicated.

B 18. I prefer to read books that provoke thought and allow the mind to wander and explore a variety of scenarios.

A 19. I'd rather follow standard operating procedures than create new ways of doing things.

A 20. I want work tasks and time expectations clearly defined before I begin a project.

B 21. I'm usually on a different wavelength than most people.

B 22. I tend to answer questions with a question in order to gather more information.

A 23. I interpret things literally rather than conceptually.

A 24. I'm more interested in the production and distribution of products rather than their design and application.

B 25. I thrive on variety and dislike repetition.

B 26. I'm a risk taker and shun the conservative approach to life.

A 27. I look for tried and proven ways to solve problems and rely on past experiences rather than wasting my time seeking new and unproven solutions.

B   28.   I enjoy listening to new ideas and exploring their potential rather than dealing with the mundane.

B   29.   I'd rather create with my mind than produce with my hands.

A   30.   When confronted with a problem, I react quickly rather than dwelling on it before doing anything.

D   31.   I will suppress my own feelings rather than hurt the feelings of others.

D   32.   I go overboard for people and overextend myself to meet their needs even at my own expense.

C   33.   I don't show my feelings easily and have been told that I'm hard to get to know.

C   34.   I'd rather deal with task problems than people problems.

C   35.   I resolve conflicts based on what is fair rather than being concerned with feelings.

D   36.   I find that people tend to take advantage of my good nature and kindheartedness.

C   37.   I react with logic rather than emotion.

C   38.   I rarely seek advice from others before I make a decision.

C   39.   I'm critical by nature and express my opinions freely.

D   40.   I warm up to people easily and wouldn't want to be thought of as cold and indifferent.

D   41.   I prefer a work environment where there's no conflict and people are appreciated and praised for what they contribute.

C   42. I make decisions based on logic rather than emotions.

D   43. I show my feelings easily.

D   44. I'm much more accepting of others than judgmental.

D   45. I expect those close to me to be sensitive to my feelings and emotional ups and downs, and I feel hurt when they're not.

D   46. I resolve conflicts by asking people for their advice so that I can gain reassurance and confidence in my decisions.

C   47. I stay calm, cool, and collected in situations where others are reacting emotionally.

D   48. I'm good at resolving people problems.

C   49. I'm a perfectionist and like things done the right way—my way.

C   50. I'm more task-oriented than people-oriented.

D   51. I'm more concerned with making good decisions than right decisions.

C   52. I'd rather work with someone who's reasonable and responsible than with someone who's thoughtful and kind.

D   53. I'm a peacemaker, not an aggressor.

D   54. I tend to be overly sympathetic to the needs of people.

C   55. I'm more interested in solving problems than dwelling on them.

C 56. I deal with people issues straightforward and call them like they are.

D 57. It is important to promote good feelings and harmony within my relationships.

C 58. I think that it's more important to be respected than to be liked.

D 59. I'm good at creating a team atmosphere and getting others to rally around a common goal or cause.

C 60. I show how much I care for someone by being responsible and conscientious rather than being emotional and sentimental.

Total the letters circled:

_____Total A's   _____Total B's
_____Total C's   _____Total D's

Add **A** and **C** together and place that total under RED.
Add **B** and **C** together and place that total under YELLOW.
Add **A** and **D** together and place that total under ORANGE.
Add **B** and **D** together and place that total under GREEN.

RED   **YELLOW**

A + C _____   B + C _____

ORANGE   **GREEN**

A + D _____   B + D _____

Interpreting the Scores

While each of us regularly uses all of the mental processes identified in the Personality Color Indicator, we're primarily driven neurologically by the mental functioning of only one of the four colors. This one color, identified through the highest score, represents your core personality trait, which again determines how you gather and process information and make decisions. This drives what motivates you, determines your inherent and instinctive behavior, and influences your perception of love.

The second-highest number and the color associated with it represent what is called your coping personality. You might find yourself using this one to fit into a world that marches to a different drummer than you. It's a reflection of your personality characteristics, meaning the behavior created by the external influences of conditioning.

If your highest numbers are in either of the colors of Green or Orange, it indicates that you make decisions based on how they feel—you use your emotions to judge whether something is right or wrong for you. If your numbers are highest in either Red or Yellow, it means that you make decisions based on logic and reasoning, and prefer the analytical approach. Should you find that you have a tie between two colors for your highest score, I suggest that you read both descriptions, highlighting what you can relate to as you go along. It will quickly become obvious what your primary color is.

Just because you have two or more numbers the same doesn't mean that you have multiple personalities. The PCI isn't an instrument for measuring psychological dysfunction; a tie just means you're flexible and adaptable or are in an intense time of change and personal growth. It's also important to keep in mind that when the color you turn out to be isn't how you see yourself, or isn't who you want to be, it may indicate that you've actually grown so accustomed to operating from your characteristics rather than your traits that you've lost sight of who you really are.

If your score is particularly high in one color, meaning that there's more than a five-point spread between your top colors, it reflects that you function primarily from your traits. So when you're required to step outside of them, you'll have to consciously make the choice to do so. If all of your numbers are close, meaning within one point of each other, it can mean you're adaptable, or you're in a time of change and unsure of the direction you should go.

It should also be noted that if your personality color is Green, it's not unusual for your numbers to be close in all categories because Greens are the chameleons of the personality world. By nature, they're so inherently flexible that they'll appear to change their colors constantly. In other words, they're very adept at taking on the personality behavior of the people they're interacting with or the behavior they feel is needed to help them complete their tasks. While this is a wonderful quality of their personality color, it's important for them to go back to their Greenness each day. This means creating activities that encourage them to just be themselves. As Kermit the Frog said, "It's not easy bein' green"— that is, unless you do wonderful things that help you discover how great it is to be Green.

Most important, if you find yourself feeling any discomfort or confusion from the results of the assessment, go back and read the descriptions of each of the four colors. This will help you uncover your traits and find your true color. It's in this kind of a situation that taking the assessment with your mate can be helpful, because they can offer their perspective of what they think or feel your personality color is without your feeling that they're judging you or trying to box you in.

Ready, Set, Go

Congratulations on your newfound identity! I'm sure that when you first started reading this book, you primarily used your name or told other people what you do for a living as a means of helping them identify who you are. And you Greens may have even shared your astrological sign in the hopes of finding other members of your color so that you could have fun and share your similar interests. Now, thanks to the PCI, you've created a whole new identity and have the distinction of belonging to one of the four unique and fabulous groups of personality colors. In addition, you also have a new way to express who you are and a means of recognizing the people in your life from this perspective.

As I describe each of the colors in the next four chapters, don't be surprised if you find yourself saying, "Oh, that's why I can't get along with that person. We aren't alike, so we don't see things the same way," or "That's why I like that person—they're like me." As you read through each type, you'll see that some have a higher need to control, some are more serious, some are more intent on keeping the peace (even at their own expense), and some are more fun loving and unpredictable. Using this knowledge as a foundation, you'll begin to understand how personality impacts the interaction between people and why the different colors have different needs.

There's an old saying that states: "We can choose our friends, but we can't choose our family." I happen to come from a family where my father and sister are Red, and my mother and brother are Green. I'm a Yellow. I can assure you that I've spent many hours trying to figure out how that happened! Yet once I learned more about how personality affects the way we perceive things, I found dealing with the dynamics of my family easier and less frustrating—both for them and for me. I realized that it wasn't their intention to be difficult or contrary—they just saw things in another way. Consequently, how they're going to react or respond to a situation is going to be different from me. If you, too, discover that your family is rich in colors, I think what you'll learn in the next few chapters will be of great value. Will it change them? Probably not. However, it *will* change how you accept and interact with them. You may even find yourself appreciating the very things about them that used to cause you so much frustration in the past. I hope that you'll find what you're about to learn not only fun, but also liberating.

A Final Thought to Ponder

> *If a man does not keep pace with his companions,*
> *perhaps it is because he hears a different drummer.*
> *Let him step to the music which he hears,*
> *however measured or far away.*

— Henry David Thoreau

CHAPTER FIVE

The Red Personality:
The "Just-Get-It-Done" People

If you were to ask Angie's parents what word best describes her, they'd most likely say <u>controlling.</u> It seems that all throughout her life, Angie has always had to be in control of everything, and when she felt she wasn't, she'd push people, or influence her environment until she gained power. After her divorce, however, she found that she was no longer in control. She was without a job and had two small children to care for.

Because of her Red personality, instead of getting caught up in her emotions and the "woe-is-me" syndrome, she sat down, made a list of her strengths, and created a plan of action for how she was going to take care of her children and herself. Then she proceeded to go out and get work. It didn't make any difference to her that she hadn't held a job in ten years. All she knew was that it was now her responsibility to take care of her family and see that all of their basic needs were met.

In her first interview, the company owner asked why he should hire her. Her response was blunt and to the point: "Because I'm good at producing results, managing time, and controlling tasks, and I want to make a lot of money—which means that <u>you'll</u> make a lot of money." Being a Red personality himself, he appreciated her straightforward and aggressive nature, and he knew she was right regarding revenue. He also recognized how much she was like him, and he liked that. He realized *that hiring her would give him the opportunity to grow his company because he'd have someone who could take over the tasks he no longer had the time or desire to do.*

Being the determined, hardworking, controlling, take-charge type of person she was, Angie quickly moved from sales into a management position, and ultimately found herself a key player in helping the owner decide the best course of action to keep the business growing and competitive.

A General Description of the Red Personality

The Red personality is the most persistent, hard-charging, controlling, aggressive, forceful, domineering, and intimidating of all of the colors. Timid they aren't, whether it's heading up a project or getting someone to do what they want. They also aren't the type to leave you guessing about what's on their mind. Reds will always let you know, in no uncertain terms, what they think about you or your actions. However, they *will* leave you in the dust if you move too slowly or are indecisive.

Reds take charge of a situation and expect others to do the same. They aren't easily intimidated and won't hesitate to bulldoze their way over anything or anyone who stands between them and their goal. The saying "Lead, follow, or get out of the way" best describes this personality type, especially once they make up their minds about what needs to be done or how to do it. A Red's perspective is that if others can't keep up with their pace or put up with their intensity, then they should stay out of the way.

Reds are logical in their decision making and rely on what's familiar, using historical precedent to help them decide *what* needs to be done and *how* it should be handled. Since they're logical, they must make sense of something before they can act upon it. They aren't abstract thinkers, nor do they get caught up in the fantasies or illusions of the mind. They're realistic, pragmatic, sensible, and down-to-earth.

They're literal in their interpretation of what's said, and they see things as either black or white. There's no gray area in their thinking—or in their lives. It either is or it isn't. A Red's perspective is that if it looks like a duck, quacks like a duck, and walks like a duck—then it's a duck. They have very little patience or tolerance for people who want to just sit around contemplating things or engage in the creation of ideas that don't seem to serve a purpose, or that they don't intend to act on.

Reds primarily focus on solving obvious problems, and they don't spend a lot of time contemplating future challenges. Because they're literal, they rely on their five senses to gather information: If they can't see, hear, touch, taste, or smell it, then it isn't real. Reds want tangible proof that something exists and aren't at all interested in theorizing. "Just the facts" is their mantra, so you'd better do your homework and be prepared to back up what you say to them. Because of their logical, straightforward approach to doing things, they're the easiest to identify of all of the four personality colors.

Reds are the "just-get-it-done" people, and they expect the same from everyone else. They pride themselves on their ability to manage time, be productive, and make their deadlines. They have zero tolerance for people who are lazy, lack initiative, or don't follow through. If a Red makes a commitment to you, from their perspective it's cast in concrete. Conversely, if you give them your word on something, it, too, is set in stone. It doesn't make any difference to them if your circumstances change—a promise is a promise. They see it as your problem and not theirs.

Reds are also very much "it's-all-about-me" people. They're demanding, impatient, self-centered, and self-serving, and can be brutally honest in expressing what they're thinking. Because of their logical, sensible nature, they appear insensitive to the other colors, but this really isn't the case—especially from a Red's perspective! It's just that they don't place the same value on emotions that some of the other personalities do. Consequently, they don't see the need to express their own emotions, and they don't think other people need to either.

For Reds, emotions are distractions and hindrances that impede progress and the problem-solving process. They don't understand why people can't just get over it when their feelings get hurt. Reds are more interested in hitting their objectives than winning popularity contests. If getting what they want and need forces them to step on a few toes, then so be it. They figure that it's the other person's problem anyway, so let them deal with it. As a matter of fact, Reds see emotional outbursts as signs of weakness, being out of control, and an inability to manage behavior.

They're not very good when it comes to saying "I'm sorry," or having to admit they're wrong. If Reds do find themselves in a position where they've made a mistake or said something hurtful, they'll usually attribute it to just being a minor misunderstanding rather than a big problem. They're not the personality type that's driven by guilt, nor do they find it necessary to explain themselves. Their aggressive, controlling nature and domineering approach can wear down many people, especially the personality colors who tend to relate and interact with their world emotionally.

Don't worry about needing to coax a Red to establish their hierarchical presence in relationships—or to share their position with others. They're born leaders who tend to run both their home and work environments in a strict, regimented, organized, and no-nonsense manner. As a result, some of the other personalities look to them to take charge and are more than happy to let them make the decisions and accept the responsibility for what happens.

Reds know what they want, and what they want is to have things their own way. They're strong willed and don't like others questioning their decisions or their authority. They're confident and aren't concerned with how other people feel about them. The need to be liked isn't what drives their behavior, and they don't view it as a measure of success. The only criteria Reds place any value on are results. Everything is measured against the bottom line. It makes no difference how hard someone tries or how much effort they expend; if the results aren't there, then the person fails in the eyes of a Red. As one Red put it in a workshop, "Effort isn't something you can take to the bank—results are."

These personalities aren't the type who easily give up control to anyone, including those they love. It's difficult for them to hand over *any* responsibility unless they're absolutely sure that they can trust the person they're delegating to—meaning that they trust them to get it done right and on time. Reds don't like to be blind-sided or caught off guard, and they don't like surprises. To ensure that none of these things happen, they tend to overcompensate by being demanding, aggressive, and domineering. It isn't unusual for Reds to create chaos, confusion, and stress because they know that other people won't want to be around them, which actually puts them in control.

The motivation behind these actions is money, power, and status, and they'll be the first ones to tell you that this is true. Their benchmarks for success are the accumulation of things. The more they own, the more expensive their toys, and the bigger their house, the more successful they feel. They also believe that tangible possessions tell other people that they're good at what they do, are good providers, and are hard workers.

Because possessions are such an integral part of their self-image, Reds live with the constant anxiety that someone is going to take away what they have or take advantage of them because they have so much. This anxiety makes them suspicious of other people's actions; and is primarily responsible for creating their insecurities, paranoia, and antagonistic behavior. If you were to confront a Red—which you might want to think twice before doing—you'd find that they're aggressive, argumentative, and quick to attack back by pointing out your inadequacies. They're not shy when it comes to letting you know that you're the one who messed things up, so you're the one who needs to fix things. Once again, it's your problem not theirs.

Reds are fiercely competitive and love the smell of victory. They see competition as one of the joys of life and approach any competitive situation with enthusiasm and vigor. Their attitude is that someone is going to lose, but it's not going to be them. However, Reds have a difficult time recognizing when it's time to quit. Consequently, they'll push themselves beyond what's healthy for their bodies and self-esteem. Reds view themselves as survivalists, and if winning is the name of the game, then it's their job to come out on top . . . no matter what it takes to do so.

Their motto is "Never give up, and full speed ahead! Damn the torpedoes!" They can be stubborn and relentless, and will move forward with brute strength if they think that's what it will take to come out the victor. If you're a personality color who doesn't deal well with confrontation, then I strongly suggest that you don't put yourself in a competitive situation with a Red.

Goals and objectives drive these individuals. They like to know what needs to be done, when it must be completed, and fully understand the ramifications if they don't meet the deadline or their goals. Success and excellence are their only options, so they'll commit whatever time and resources are needed in order to accomplish both. The way Reds approach attaining their goals is to create a game plan that includes gathering only the pertinent facts, reviewing the options, evaluating what's been done before and whether it worked, and then driving themselves and other people to make sure it happens.

Failure isn't an option to Reds. They'll take whatever action is needed, even if it means assuming an aggressive posture or using intimidation. If you're paired with a Red mate, I'm sure you know what I mean and have experienced the behaviors described.

Ten Observable Behavioral Traits of a Red Personality

Here are ten of the most predictable and observable behavioral traits of the Red personality. Each of these traits contributes to their strong-willed nature and their take-charge persona. Although other personality colors may display what appears to be similar behaviors, a person who's a Red will demonstrate them more consistently and frequently.

1. Controlling. Being in control is everything—and the only thing—for a Red. Their take-charge personality and ability to oversee people and tasks makes them natural-born leaders and comfortable with the responsibility that comes with this leadership. As a means of gaining control of a situation, Reds will raise their voices, become physically explosive, and use whatever behavioral tactics are necessary to ensure that other people don't challenge them or question their authority.

2. Competitive. They're neither hesitant, squeamish, nor faint-hearted when it comes to doing whatever it takes to win. They're not the type of personality to cheer for the underdog; they want to associate with winners. Even in their love relationships, Reds tend to create competitive situations by challenging their mate to come up with the best date, or plan the best weekend getaway. They'll even reward their mate with gifts in order to inspire participation.

3. Process driven. Reds believe that the only way to move forward with anything is in a sequential, step-by-step, logical manner. They understand the need for rules and procedures because for them it's the only way to maintain control and ensure that goals and objectives are met. Reds pride themselves on their productiveness and see repetition, redundancy, and routine as just part of the process of getting from point A to point B.

4. Hot-tempered. The volatility of the Red's temper makes itself known quickly and frequently. Their explosive nature can be intimidating, unsettling, and catch people off guard, thus causing others to become submissive and timid. Temperamental outbursts are the Red's way of gaining control over a situation and preventing others from challenging their authority. Depending on their level of frustration or degree of anger, these emotional displays may range from yelling to throwing objects to hitting something or someone. The difficulty other people experience when dealing with Reds who are angry is not knowing how violent their outbursts will be or how long they'll last.

5. Orderly. Reds need to be organized and live an orderly life in order to be okay and feel good about themselves. They're sometimes described using the terms *drill sergeant* and *taskmaster* because of their need for control, cleanliness, and tidiness. They have a very difficult time living with emotional turmoil, chaos, or clutter. Reds want everything in its proper place and expect others to put things where they belong. They're the ultimate list makers and use productivity aids such as daily schedules, personal digital assistants (PDAs), and cell phones with calendars to help man-age their lives, minimize chaos, and prevent things from falling through the cracks.

6. Pragmatic. These individuals have dogged determination and are relentless in their drive to be productive. Reds approach everything in a no-nonsense, straightforward, matter-of-fact way. They take all tasks and projects seriously, and instinctively look for the most efficient way of doing things. They're hardheaded and hard-nosed and won't take no for an answer. They're demanding both of themselves and of other people.

7. Conscientious. Whether it's satisfying the demands of their employers or fulfilling the needs of their families, Reds are willing to do whatever it takes to get the job done. They're dedicated, reli-able, diligent, and intensely focused. They won't stop until they get what they want, and no matter what they do or take on, they always strive to do their best. Reds see it as their responsibility to provide for those they love and to see that all their basic needs are met. They think that they're the best qualified to do that—and in fact, the only ones who can.

8. Realistic. Reds are down-to-earth and have their feet plant-ed firmly on the ground. They're sensible and realistic—no pie in the sky or head in the clouds for them. They see things as they really are versus what they'd like them to be. Reds conduct their lives by living the cliché that "what you see is what you get." They don't have the time or inclination to create things that aren't practical or that don't fill an immediate need, and they don't jump on ideas or schemes that have no basis for producing the results they want.

9. Resistant to change. The Red personality will fight change tooth and nail if they can't see how it will benefit them. They'd rather stay with what's tried-and-true than taking a chance on something new. They're not the type of people who embrace change just because someone else tells them that they must or that it's the right thing to do. Reds want to see the facts that support the *need* for change, and then they want a guarantee that if they do change, it will work. They take a wait-and-see attitude, and unless they can minimize the risks, they'll dig their heels in and stay with what they know has worked in the past.

10. Predictable. Reds are the most predictable of all of the personality colors, and this quality shows up in every aspect of their lives: their daily routines, lifestyle, how they adhere to the rules, and how they consistently strive to do what's right. Even the way they comb their hair and their styles of clothes tend to remain constant. Everything they do has some kind of history behind it, meaning that they've done it or tried it before. Whether it's working or playing, Reds establish schedules and form habits that drive what they do and when and how they do it.

What Love Means to a Red

Reds take love very seriously and define it as being conditional: They'll give you their love if you'll take care of their needs first. Consequently, they have a lot of expectations for their relationships. For Reds, love has rules that must be followed to ensure that the relationship moves forward in a positive manner, and they're full of shoulds and shouldn'ts. This means that Reds have to feel safe and secure before they're willing to share how they feel or show affection. The first rule is that their mate must be willing to put their own needs on the back burner. The Reds' inherent need to take care of those they love makes them good mates. However, they show their concern by being controlling. This can be difficult to live with because they're continually demanding time and activity accountability.

Reds are traditionalists when it comes to love and conventional in how they divide duties and tasks. They tend to use stereotypical gender roles in determining who should do what and how affection should be expressed. They also expect their mate to share in the responsibilities and to work as hard as they do in building a secure, predictable life together. Reds demonstrate their love by seeing that their mate's basic needs are met, including food, shelter, transportation, and clothing. For Reds, this says "I love you."

In general, this personality isn't one to overindulge those they care for or be too sentimental. They'll usually wait for a special occasion to express how they feel and show it through gifts. However, don't always expect them to remember those red-letter days! If you're not getting the obvious signs that they recall the special dates, you might find you'll have to remind them. Don't read this as meaning that they don't care, because they do. It's just that their attention is usually focused more on work demands or other responsibilities rather than your birthday or anniversary.

It's also helpful to tell the Red what you'd like in the way of a gift. This takes the pressure off them having to guess what you might want and possibly buying the wrong thing, and Reds don't like to be wrong about anything. It also ensures that you'll get exactly what you want.

There's an interesting dichotomy in this kind of situation: Reds don't like to be told what to do and will become angry when someone tries to tell them. Yet in the case of buying gifts for special occasions, they really appreciate the help, and will even go so far as letting you tell them exactly where to shop. When you plant the seeds in their mind, they'll have the time to think about it, and suddenly it will become *their* idea. Then buying that gift for you makes them feel good about themselves, and you get what you want. It's a win-win for everybody.

For the most part, Reds keep their emotions bottled up inside and will only express them if they're pressed to do so. This doesn't mean that they don't have feelings (because they do), and it shouldn't be misinterpreted that they don't need love or want their mate to share their affection. Reds like to hear the words *I love you,* even if they don't flow easily from their own mouths.

People in this color think that their feelings for others are obvious because of the things they do for them, and just assume that their mate knows how much they're loved. Consequently, they don't find it necessary to say "I love you." Now that's fine if you're a Red partnered with a Red, but what happens when you're a different personality color and need to hear those words regularly? Unfortunately, there's a very good chance that won't happen— that is unless you *tell them* you need to hear "I love you" more often. Then they'll comply because they know that if you get what you need, then they'll get what they need, too.

Reds are possessive of their mate's time and attention and expect them to always be there. As a result, they tend to create love relationships that foster dependency and support compliant behavior. Their insecurities arise when they feel "unsafe" and think that their mate isn't supportive. Their anger surfaces when they think that their partner isn't carrying their weight or when they feel that their mate is taking advantage of them.

While Reds are excellent problem solvers at work or dealing with other people's conflicts, they have a difficult time fixing their own lives. Reds find it easier to avoid issues altogether rather than stepping up to them. It isn't unlike this color to create a bunch of petty problems just so they don't have to deal with a real one. They figure that if they create enough other distractions, then maybe the problem will take care of itself or will just go away on its own.

It's also interesting to note that Reds don't intentionally avoid conflict at work, but they do at home. When there's trouble in the relationship and angry words have been exchanged, it's very uncomfortable and unsettling for Reds. They find it easier to avoid their mate by working longer hours or busying themselves with other things than having to spend time quarrelling or hashing things out over and over again. It's easy to recognize when Reds are feeling inadequate in the love department: They'll compensate by being overly controlling, go into avoidance, or step outside the relationship to get what they need.

Reds like being their own people and value their individuality and autonomy. Consequently, they aren't interested in being with someone who tries to control them. They like their relationships to involve both separateness and togetherness, and truthfully, more time apart. Reds don't have the need to share everything with their mate, yet they want their mate to share everything with them; they don't want to do everything with their mate, but they want their mate to want to do everything with them.

It sounds like they want to have their cake and eat it, too. Well, that's true, because love for the Red is having the best of both worlds: a companion who shares their interests and wants to be with them, and the freedom to do what they want when they want to. Again, it goes back to the Reds wanting to write the rules and then expecting their mates to follow them. This means that if your mate is a Red personality, there will be times when you'll be included and times when you won't. From the Red's perspective, it isn't personal and doesn't mean they don't love you. It's just that there will be occasions when being with their friends will be more important than being with you.

The Reds' Expression of Love's Many Splendors

Romance

Being romantic must serve a purpose for Reds. They view romantic gestures as initiating desire and triggering the biological need for physical contact. Reds enjoy being the recipient of romantic interludes because their ego gets fed and they feel important and desirable. They get the message that they're appreciated, loved, and sexually attractive. However, Reds are conservative when it comes to romance and will become uncomfortable with gestures that are excessive, are too touchy-feely, or require them to act in a way that's unnatural for their normal behavior. These demonstrations are more of a distraction and a turnoff rather than a turn-on.

The kind of romantic activities Reds like best are those that are familiar, such as having their mate fix their favorite meal, sitting together watching their favorite movie or television program, or going out to dinner at their favorite restaurant.

While Reds enjoy being romanced, they aren't known for lavishly showering their mate with gallantry in return. It usually takes a special occasion to trigger their romantic spirit and initiate the outreach. Here again, they're conventional, meaning that they'll send flowers, give a nice card, buy a box of candy, pick up tickets to a favorite concert or sports event, and do thoughtful things like going to a coffee shop or running errands so that their mate will have more time to relax.

When Reds use gifts as a means of expressing themselves romantically, the presents tend to be more on the practical side rather than being extravagant. They don't like to waste money on things that don't fill a need or serve a purpose. The gifts they buy have two purposes: They show their mate how much they're valued and let other people how much their mate is valued. Consequently, it's not unusual for the Red to buy their mate a new car or an expensive piece of jewelry, give them season sports tickets, or take an expensive vacation on those really important special occasions.

A Red's need for staying with what's familiar shows up in this department, meaning that the romantic interludes they like best are those that are repeated year after year. In their minds, the security that comes from staying with something familiar is comforting and seems to somehow add to the specialness of being together. It also reduces the potential for stress and takes away the anxiety that comes from having to deal with the unknown. From their perspective, why try something new if you already have something that works? Remember, Reds don't like surprises, even when it comes to romance.

Passion

As with romance, passion for the Reds is an integral step in their preparation for sharing physical pleasure. Passion allows them to express themselves through their sexuality and through the sensations of their body. They see passionate gestures as those that entice and stimulate the five physical senses: sight, hearing, touch, taste, and smell. However, they can run both hot and cold when it comes to passion. When their passion button is turned on, their expression is robust, lusty, raw, and almost animalistic; and how they use their body to express their desire is intense, meaning you won't have to guess whether they're turned on or not.

When that button isn't turned on, they're passionately docile, behaviorally compliant, emotionally indifferent, and aren't interested in engaging in sizzling foreplay. This is usually an indicator that they aren't feeling good about themselves or that they're mentally overburdened with problems. Using passion as an indicator to read the Red is a good way to tell how they're feeling about themselves and the relationship, whether they're interested in sex or even interested in you, and where they are mentally.

Intimacy

In general, being intimate is difficult for Reds because they aren't really sure what it means or what's required from them in order to qualify as intimacy. Common definitions of this splendor describe it as being private and personal, attached, inseparable, the sharing of emotions, emotional closeness, and using words that express deep feelings and endearment. Yet when we look at the overall behavior of Reds, we'll see that many of these qualities aren't necessarily ones that Reds display, nor are they part of their inherent interaction with people.

It isn't easy for Reds to bare their souls, express how they feel deep inside, or open up to others and leave themselves emotionally vulnerable. Intimacy, for the most part, requires an openness and expressiveness that they don't deal with well. It implies lowering the veil and letting others see beneath their take-charge and always-in-control persona, and that's something a Red doesn't have any interest in doing.

A Red's perception of intimacy is spending time with one another, building a future together, and exchanging sexual pleasures. It's not being emotional or sharing feelings, but it does mean being close and personal. Intimacy is important to Reds and is vital if they're going to remain engaged in the relationship. They see it as increasing the pleasure of sex, enhancing the enjoyment of being together, and adding an element of contentment to the relationship. Intimacy fosters the loyalty they need from their mate; it creates certainty and adds an unspoken value to their union. It helps them feel good about who they are and about their choice of a mate.

Reds express their intimacy through words of endearment and via material goods, such as the gifts they give and the things they do. Verbal expressions include the use of pet names that either have a sentimental meaning or form a favorable image of their mate in their mind. When a Red uses a nickname, they're telling the other person how much they care for them and how desirable they are.

If we were to look at the four expressions of intimacy—physical, emotional, mental, and spiritual—a Red will usually rank physical intimacy as the most important and emotional the least. The former allows them to express their love through the exchange of sexual pleasures, while the latter makes them vulnerable to criticism and opens the door for their mate to point out their inadequacies. They really don't see emotional intimacy as adding value, but instead believe that it creates problems and adds to the complexity of making a relationship work.

Sex

Reds are driven by their physical needs, and their primary desires are for sex and food. So if you aren't in the mood for sex . . . what's for dinner? This holds true for both men and women of this color. To them, this physical connection is a necessity of life. They see it as a true indicator of how they're feeling about their relationship. When they want sex, things are good. When they don't, there's something going on with their partner that needs to be addressed or changed. Reds see sex as serving several purposes: It helps them relax, satisfies their biological needs, provides an opportunity to express their sexuality, makes them feel good about themselves, and shows their mate that they're loved.

Reds want sex on a regular basis—like every day. So if too many days or weeks go by without it, their behavior becomes aggressive, their attitude surly, and their view of the relationship takes a nosedive. When it comes to intercourse, they're primarily focused on filling their own needs. Consequently, while they want their mate to enjoy the process, they don't feel responsible for that person's sexual satisfaction. Now, as harsh as that may sound, and as difficult as it might be for other personality colors to accept deep down inside, sex centers around fulfilling their needs, wants, and desires—just like everything else.

Reds do enjoy foreplay up to a point, but if it goes on for too long they get bored and are ready to move on. They see it as a way to help get their mate aroused and as a means of helping themselves mentally shift gears so that they can focus on the desires and needs of the body. Just as in the rest of their lives, Reds tend to stick with what's familiar, comfortable, and proven to work. Their tendency isn't to initiate new experiences or be overly creative. They'll stick with the same positions and the same activities for foreplay. However, this doesn't mean they aren't open and receptive to trying new things—it's just that if you're their partner, you'll have to be the initiator. Keep in mind that they don't like surprises, so tell them what you're going to do and how you're going to make them feel. This gives them time to warm up to the idea and helps them get comfortable with what's going to happen. Talking about sex is a real turn-on to them.

Since satisfying their biological needs is such an integral part of what makes them feel good about themselves, the absence of sexual intercourse takes a real toll on their relationship and undermines how they feel about their mate. When the physical intimacy ceases to exist, it isn't unusual for Reds to move outside of their relationship to fulfill their sexual needs. Should this happen and they're confronted about their affairs, they'll often still profess their love for their mate or say, "I don't love the other person, I love you. I just had sex with them, nothing more." Reds say this because they don't see sex and love as being one and the same—or for that matter needing one to have the other. Reds will also seek sexual gratification with others when their relationship has become too emotionally volatile and unpredictable.

Red males measure themselves on their sexual performance in the same way they measure their performance in their favorite sport. If they feel that they did well, they'll give themselves high marks, and if they think that it wasn't up to par, they'll make excuses about it. Sexual performance both for the Red male and female is greatly impacted by what's happening mentally or physically. Rarely is it affected by emotional concerns. If their mind is burdened with problems or overwhelmed with too much to do, their desire for sex decreases. If they're too tired, have had too much alcohol, or are experiencing physical discomfort, it will be difficult for them to stay focused on the process. While drinking and driving is never a good thing, neither is drinking too much and then trying to have sex.

The bottom line when it comes to sex is this: Reds need it physically and mentally. They want their mate to be ready, willing, and able when they are.

Communication

Communication isn't one of this color's greatest virtues, nor are they very tolerant and patient with the process. This is because the process requires both listening and talking, and Reds—whether introverted or extroverted—are more interested in talking. They're just waiting for the opportunity to give advice and tell other people how to do things. However, there are some exceptions. They'll be open to listening to what others have to say if it means they'll get their way, if you're discussing what interests them, or if it sounds like you know what you're talking about. But don't misinterpret listening as meaning that they agree with you, because that may not be the case.

Reds will listen as a way of determining what position you're taking, and then they'll share their own perspective. Usually it will be opposite from yours, as they enjoy playing devil's advocate. It also helps to keep in mind that listening skills tend to differ from one personality color to another. In the case of the Reds, most of the time that others are talking, they're actually thinking about the next thing they're going to say, and the minute they get what they want to say formulated in their minds, they open their mouth. Out it will come, even if it means interrupting. In their mind, they haven't cut anyone off, they're just trying to help others get back on track and ensuring that the facts are straight.

Small talk, conversations based on unfounded speculation, or discussions dealing with emotional issues are irritating and a waste of time from a Red's perspective. So is anything involving brainstorming. They're not interested in engaging in meetings or discussions, whether at work or at home, where there isn't some sort of action plan to implement what's created. Reds see the communication process as needing to serve a purpose, go somewhere, and be productive. They want to talk about things that are practical, tangible, measurable, and center around their own interests. The minute they decide that a conversation isn't going where they think it should, they'll jump in and redirect it, or they'll get up and leave the room. It seems that their need to be in control even applies to the communication process.

Reds enjoy discussions that focus on making things happen and activities involving planning, such as upcoming vacations, their future, how to manage their finances, when to buy a new car or house, when to retire, and what they'll do after they stop working. They're not interested in sitting around talking about problems or gossiping. Even though Reds want to be included in conversations, don't expect them to openly volunteer anything about themselves. You'll probably have to pull the information out of them or wait until you're having dinner with friends to find out what's really happening in their lives. The reason why Reds share so openly with friends is because they don't feel that they have to be accountable to that group. Consequently, they'll open up, and you'll get the entire scoop.

Reds are blunt, straightforward, frank, and matter-of-fact in their communication style. Their hallmark is saying it like it is without mincing words or worrying about whether they'll step on toes or hurt someone's feelings in the process. When something you're doing is bothering them, or if they're unhappy with you, you'll know it because they'll tell you. They don't leave you guessing.

Reds interpret things literally. What they hear is what they believe and what they'll act on. Words become cast in concrete once spoken, and they'll hold you to whatever you've said. So if you're going to use a Red as a sounding board, be sure to tell them that that's what you're doing. Otherwise, they'll quickly jump in and begin to solve your problems—whether you have any or not. Or worse yet, they'll start giving you advice on how to handle a situation or person before you've even had time to think about it. The real clincher in conversations where you're just mulling things over is that they'll expect you to follow through on the advice they give you, even though that's not what you wanted or needed.

Commitment

Commitment creates the security and stability a Red needs in order to feel good about their choice of a mate and their relationship. It's important to them, and they take it very seriously. Consequently, they see a commitment as being forever. Even though Reds want to hold on to their independence and autonomy, at some point in their lives being single becomes negative and they find themselves wanting to share their time with someone—but they aren't the type to impulsively choose the first person who comes along.

Reds want to make sure that their partner will take good care of them and appreciate what they offer. As a result, they're careful, cautious, and guarded about whom they'll let in their lives. They'd rather take a "wait-and-see" position than make a costly mistake that ends up with their being mismatched. Reds begin evaluating the person on the very first date to see if they'd be a good spouse and parent. If they feel safe with the person and believe their needs will be met, then they'll be willing to invest the money, time, and energy necessary to develop a long-term relationship. If they decide that the person won't fit their needs, then they usually won't go beyond the first date—unless the sex is particularly good.

How Love Changes with Age

While what love means to the Red changes with age—their intensity wanes—their need for physical contact and sex doesn't. Around age 40, Reds begin to mellow, and their need to control everything and everybody both at home and work seems to become less important. Their patience for their mate's idiosyncrasies increases as they recognize that it's just the way they are. Besides, they begin to realize that it will take too much effort to try to change the other person. When they reach this point, Reds become more tolerant and accepting of the differences between themselves and their mate and are less inclined to try to manipulate their partner into doing things. With age comes the awareness that their mate has probably learned how to turn off the Red's rhetoric and will disregard it anyway. At this stage in life, the Red figures why waste the time or the energy, so they reconcile themselves to the fact there are some things they can change and some they can't.

Around age 50, they begin to step back and look at their life and find themselves questioning whether what they did with the first half had any meaning and if they impacted other people's lives positively. Their emotional insecurities surface as they realize that they aren't the spring chicken they used to be. They question what's really important and start to develop a softer and gentler side of themselves. They become more attentive, thoughtful, and supportive toward their mate, and their relationship takes on a new importance, as does their desire to spend more time with their partner.

Reds begin to need a stronger emotional bond with their children and want to see them more during this time. The problem is that by the time they reach this stage in life, their children are grown and busy doing their own things. This can leave a Red wondering where the time went and questioning if what they did was worth it. It can also make them melancholy, depressed, and feeling as if life has passed them by.

Age 60 is a turning point for Reds, as they find themselves entering a new phase in their life: retirement. No more having to put up with other people's problems, responsibility for their children, or being accountable to those they don't care about. Suddenly, life becomes more appealing because they're free to do what they want, when they want. They begin to understand more about who they really are and recognize that it was their love for their mate and family that drove them to work as hard as they did—and that providing for their loved ones brought the greatest satisfaction. When they realize that they were motivated by affection rather than just making money, their perception of love takes on a new meaning. They feel good about themselves and welcome the opportunity to enjoy life and fall in love with their mate all over again.

Reds' Fears, Insecurities, and Anxieties

It's difficult to believe when you watch a Red personality in action, assuming leadership roles, taking charge of situations, and aggressively making things happen that they have insecurities and suffer from anxieties. However, under that strong outer persona of aggression and self-confidence is someone who deals with these kinds of emotional issues:

- Fear of not being able to provide adequately for those they love

- Fear of being emotionally vulnerable

- Fear of failure

- Fear of poverty

- Anxieties around being out of control

- Frustration at not being able to control their environment and the actions of others

- Fear of losing what they have—they'd rather stay in a bad relationship than make a change that could potentially jeopardize their financial security or cause them to lose their possessions

- Insecurities that stem from feeling that they don't belong or have a place to call home—this is an ongoing problem even if they do have a home and are secure in their relationship

- Fear of personal rejection

- Fear of intimacy

- Sexual-performance anxiety

- Avoidance of emotional needs and development

- Fear of being rendered powerless

The Evolutionary Stage of a Relationship That Reds Are Most Attracted To

When it comes to what evolutionary stage Reds are most attracted to, it must be the dating stage, hands down, because that's where love is exciting and the sex is good. In this stage, the element of responsibility for having to take care of someone else hasn't surfaced yet. They can still be rowdy and self-indulgent, and enjoy time sharing their favorite interests without concern for what the other person thinks about them. Their attitude is "take it or leave it," and "what you see is what you get." In the dating stage, they're still free to come and go as they please and do what they want when they want, and they don't have to answer to anyone.

The Evolutionary Stage of a Relationship That's the Most Difficult for Reds

The evolutionary stage that's the most difficult for a Red is growing together as a couple. This is because their sense of responsibility takes over, and the excitement of falling in love is replaced with the burdens of having to take care of someone else. They experience a loss of identity, and their freedom is curtailed. They find themselves having to deal with emotional issues and personality differences, neither of which is their idea of fun. Then when you add job responsibilities and money problems to the dynamics of their relationship, it takes a lot of effort and focus for them to keep the flames of passion burning strong. It's difficult to keep the demands of life from snuffing out their desire for the splendors of love.

Overview of the Red Personality	
Basic needs:	• Control of both environment and people • Staying with what's familiar and proven to work • Structure and organization • Relationships that aren't emotionally demanding
Emotional needs:	• Appreciation for what they do • Sexual fulfillment • Shared interests • Participation in family decisions
Key strengths:	• Take-charge attitude • Responsible, dependable, and committed to those they love • Competitive and strong willed • Stable, consistent, and predictable
Key weaknesses:	• Overbearing and domineering • Stubborn • Intolerant of personality differences • Living in the past

Overview of the Red Personality, cont'd.	
Primary fear:	• Losing what they've acquired
Attracted to people who are:	• Supportive, attentive, submissive, compliant, predictable, fun, and easygoing
Dislike people who are:	• Arrogant and strongly opinioned • Lazy and unwilling to take responsibility for their actions • Takers rather than givers
Relationship expectations:	• Loyalty, devotion, and fidelity • Having their needs put first
Value in a relationship:	• Consistency, steadfastness, and permanence
Room for improvement:	• Increasing emotional sensitivity to their mate's needs • Listening with understanding • Developing more patience and tolerance for people who differ from them and don't share the same perspectives
Annoyances:	• Other people wasting their time
Causes of stress:	• Feeling out of control
Relationship challenge:	• Staying in love and growing together as a couple

Hot Tips for Dealing with Reds	
Love	Tell them how much you appreciate their working so hard and express your gratitude for their taking such good care of you.
Romance	If you want a romantic getaway, tell them. Don't drop hints—they don't like it.
Passion	Flirt with them and tell them how much you desire their body.
Sex	Ask them if there's anything new that they'd like to try.
Communication	Just stick to the facts and be prepared to back them up. Don't ramble on or become emotional.

Helpful Hints for Reds in Dealing with Other Personality Colors	
Love	It's important to say "I love you." Don't assume that your mate doesn't need to hear the words.
Romance	Don't wait for a special occasions to be romantic. Make a date for no particular reason and send a card, flowers, or just a note that says, "Can't wait to be with you."
Passion	Kiss them on the back of the neck and tell them how much they turn you on.
Sex	Turn sex into a romantic gesture—for example, place a rose on their pillow.
Communication	Listen and respond with empathy.

CHAPTER SIX

The Orange Personality:
The "Let's-All-Get-Along" People

*T*he best words to describe Nathan are warm, friendly, nice, considerate, polite, gentle, and sensitive. The underlying motivation that
drives his interactions with people is his inherent desire to see that their
emotional needs are met and that they're happy. As a result, he tends to
get so involved in helping others that he forgets to take care of himself.
His perception is that his needs are less important than others', so he
tends to put his life on the back burner. When I talked to Nathan about
this tendency, I asked him if it's been a problem for him. He quickly acknowledged that it has been. Then he added, "I get so caught up in other
people's emotional dramas that I can't seem to tell whether the trouble
is mine or theirs." He also said that he wished other people would appreciate all that he does for them. He remarked, "A little gratitude would
go a long way."

Professionally, Nathan is a business coach, which on the surface
sounds like a great job for his Orange personality, because it supports
his need to help people. However, part of his job is to listen to other
people's concerns and problems while creating an environment where
they can safely and confidentially vent their frustrations and anger. In
other words, he's their sounding board, which might be easy for other personality colors, but is both difficult and emotionally painful for

Oranges. It's so tough because they don't deal well with the emotional elements that come with problems, and being around displays of anger is discomforting to them. Oranges are peacemakers and will avoid any situation where the potential for strife exists. Conflict-charged environments create a tremendous amount of stress for them. I think Nathan summed it up best when he said, "I just wish everyone could get along and just work together. The world would be a better place if that could happen."

While he kept repeating that he enjoyed his work, he did admit that his job took an emotional toll on him and created an enormous amount of anxiety and guilt. When I asked him to explain, he said that he continually feels bad when he isn't able to give his clients the answers they're looking for, and feels guilty if he isn't there for them. I asked him why, and he went on to explain how his customers' needs weren't always driven by the clock, and their problems didn't only happen during the work week. Nathan believed that his job was to be there when they needed him, no matter what the time of day or day of the week. His perception was that he was on call 24/7.

When asked how his wife and family felt about this, he replied, "My wife isn't happy about it at all, and has told me that I need to set some boundaries." He shared how the situation was creating a tremendous amount of tension between them and how she even suggested that if he couldn't set some boundaries, he should get out of the field. This was very distressing because it made him feel as if he were trapped between a rock and a hard place. He loved his family <u>and</u> his job.

Nathan revealed that being in this position made him feel so bad about himself that it was emotionally debilitating and was undermining his self-esteem. He talked about how anxious he felt because it was once again time for his clients to evaluate his performance and make suggestions about how he could better serve them. Even though he knew that feedback is important, it was still something he really dreaded because his perception was that it represented criticism. He began worrying about what they'd say weeks before the evaluation process. Then if there was any form of criticism, whether constructive or not, he felt devastated and distraught, and his self-worth plummeted. He admitted that the last time it happened, it actually took him weeks to recover.

A General Description for the Orange Personality

The Orange personality is the most emotionally sensitive and volatile of all the colors. Helping other people and seeing that their emotional needs are met is what adds meaning to the Orange's life. It gives them a sense of belonging and purpose. The Orange motto is *If you're happy, then I'm happy,* and they truly mean it. When an Orange asks you how you're feeling, they're not just being courteous or polite; they're really interested. They're taking your emotional pulse to see if you're okay or distressed. This question also lets them get a sense of whether the environment is friendly or charged with conflict.

Their emotional sensitivity is expressed in their sympathetic and compassionate nature. They can actually experience what other people are feeling and have a very strong need to emotionally comfort them. The Orange's outreach is sincere and genuine; they aren't fair-weather friends. They'll be there when you're happy, feeling down, in need of help, overwhelmed emotionally, and convinced that your world is crumbling all around you. In other words, they'll share the good times and the bad, and will always be there to support you.

Oranges are the ultimate caregivers. They're devoted, committed, loyal, and self-sacrificing. In the hierarchy of their need to take care of others, the Orange's family ranks at the top of the list; then comes friends, church, community, and co-workers. At the bottom of the list, they rank themselves and their own needs. If you ask an Orange what they do for themselves, the common answer is "When?" Immediately following this response is a look that causes you to wonder why you'd even ask such a silly question. Oranges will tell you that they don't have any time for themselves because their lives are so centered around juggling the demands of family, work, and social activities. By the time they try to do something for themselves, they're either too tired or someone else needs something.

It always surprises Oranges—and even disappoints them—when the same courtesies they instinctively give to others aren't reciprocated. They expect their mate and those they love to be there for them and to return the caring, sensitivity, and under-standing. When they don't get the same emotional support that they provide others, Oranges feel unloved, unsupported, betrayed, and abandoned; they experience a deep emotional hurt. They can't understand what they've done so wrong that others don't care about them.

One of the main reasons Oranges don't get the outreach they want is that they don't ask for it. In their mind, they feel they shouldn't have to ask someone to express how much they care because that person should just do it automatically. A second rea-son they don't get what they need emotionally is that when it's offered, they'll brush it off, act as though it's not a big deal, or imply that it isn't important. Unfortunately for the Orange, the other personality colors read this as meaning that there's no need to waste time verbalizing their affection.

Oranges make taking care of people look so effortless that we tend to take what they do for granted. Consequently, we don't always show our appreciation and reach out to them when they're in need of a little tender loving care. We forget to acknowledge how their supportive nature significantly adds to the quality of our lives. Oranges don't require a lot of praise or recognition for what they do, but they do need to be appreciated for who they are and what they bring to the relationship. If we can just remem-ber, then their willingness to love us will remain foremost in their heart, and caring for our needs will stay at the top of their list.

The Orange personality feels the most secure about themselves and their life when they're in a love relationship that's both emo-tionally and financially stable, because that's how they measure their self-worth. How they perceive themselves is in direct corre-lation to how they view their connection to their partner. When they're feeling valued, appreciated, and loved, they like them-selves, their outlook on life is optimistic, and their disposition is pleasant. They're enjoyable to be around and loving them is easy.

On the other hand, if they aren't feeling good about their rela-tionship, they're moody and pensive, their outlook on life is nega-tive, their disposition is sour, and their behavior will alternate be-tween passive and aggressive—one minute they're not speaking to you, and the next minute you *wish* they weren't speaking to you. The saying, "Ain't Mama happy, ain't nobody happy," applies to both male and female Oranges.

Since who they are and how they feel about themselves is so tied to their relationship, Oranges will often use their roles within it as a means of helping other people identify with them. It isn't unusual to hear an Orange say, "I'm so-and-so's wife [or mother, or husband or father]." It's almost as if they lose their own identity when they enter into a relationship and take on that of the parts they play.

The Orange's need to have a partner is so strong that it sometimes drives them into an alliance that isn't necessarily a healthy one for either party. When this happens, it isn't unusual for either emotional or physical abuse to occur, or for the Orange to become withdrawn and submissive. Their need to be loved often causes them to stay in a bad situation, when in reality they should get out.

Part of the reason they stay is that they can't cope emotionally with the thought of being alone. The other reason is that they'd rather stay where they are than have to deal with their fear of abandonment. Without a love relationship, Oranges feel dissatisfied, incomplete, powerless, and detached from life, and their ability to feel good about themselves is a constant struggle. As a way of compensating for how they're feeling, it isn't unusual for Oranges to reach out to those in need. Consequently, they're the champions of the underdogs and the protectors of the downtrodden. They're passionate about seeing that other people don't have to put up with the abuses they do and will offer time, money, and emotional support if they believe they can make a difference in someone else's life.

Oranges don't deal well with conflict and have a difficult time functioning where there's constant tension and arguments. Emotionally volatile environments keep them off balance and undermine their ability to care for those they love. In conflict-charged situations, Oranges want to know what's expected of them, and once they figure this out they'll work hard to see that those expectations are met. When that isn't enough, they become frustrated, anxious, and domineering.

Unlike the Red personality, who will vent their anger and frustration and then move on, the Orange will "stuff" how they're feeling until it reaches a point where they can't keep it bottled up inside any longer. When this happens, there won't be any doubt that they've had all they can take. Their emotional outburst will be so explosive that it will leave you trembling like a deer caught in headlights. You'll stand there stunned and paralyzed, asking yourself how you got to that place and what happened. Their release of pent-up emotions can be so venomous that it leaves others completely shocked. There are ways to keep this from happening. However, it means heightening your sensitivity to their personality needs, telling them on a regular basis how much you appreciate all they do for you, and making the time to let them share how they're feeling.

The world of the Orange is driven by their emotions and how they react to their experiences and interactions with people. They're emotionally binary, meaning that things are always good or bad, right or wrong, pleasant or unpleasant. They're either on top of the world, or they're down in the dumps. There aren't any gray areas when it comes to how they feel about something—or about you. Since the Orange is so emotionally rigid in their judgments, other personality colors see them as difficult people to live with and be around. Others feel that they can't trust an Orange to be truthful, because what they say they're feeling on the surface isn't necessarily what's going on inside. These people are very good at putting up facades that tell others everything is fine when it really isn't. Their unpredictable emotional states can make them caring, sensitive, and giving one moment; and critical, tense, and unforgiving the next.

One of the greatest challenges for Oranges is managing anxiety. They're the true worriers of the personality world—they do it all the time. They fret about anything and everything, and sometimes don't even know why or what's really bothering them. They worry about finances, whether they're loved, whether they're doing what's expected of them, how they're going to accomplish everything, and if they're acting right. They even worry about what total strangers are thinking about them. They constantly live with the emotional anxiety that other people aren't going to like them or are going to become angry with them.

Guilt is another major issue for Oranges. They tend to hang on to past hurts longer than any other personality color. It isn't unusual for Oranges, as adults, to still be struggling with feelings of guilt that were created when they were children. Because this is such a natural part of this color's emotional makeup, they often fail to recognize how it causes them to do things they really don't want to and stay in relationships they really want to leave. They don't see how this emotion distorts their perspective, turns their desire to care for others into an obligation, and takes away the "warm and fuzzy" feeling they look for when they put the needs of others before their own.

Oranges are the organizational and administrative masters of the personality world. Their ability to manage details, deal with people issues, and handle loose ends makes them a very desirable color to have in our lives. Their need to please and make people feel comfortable coupled with their ability to anticipate the likes and dislikes of the other personalities makes them great social planners. Then when you add their need to take care of people, you have the perfect qualities of a great host or hostess. As a matter of fact, one way to identify an Orange personality is to pay attention to how they entertain. They're the ones who'll usually call their guests to find out what kinds of foods they like or if they have any dietary restrictions. Then armed with this information, they'll work hard to accommodate those needs by seeing that each person feels cared for and welcome. This holds true for both the male and female Oranges. Their idea of happiness is spending time with those they care about, serving good food and drink, and enjoying conversation.

Ten Observable Behavioral Traits of the Orange Personality

Here are ten of the most noticeable behavioral traits of an Orange personality. Each one of these helps them fulfill their innermost desire, which is to help and take care of other people.

Although other personality colors may display what appears to be similar behavior, a person who is Orange will demonstrate them more consistently and frequently.

1. Cooperative. Oranges are cooperative and respectful of those in authority. They function best in environments where teamwork is encouraged and people are sensitive to the feelings and needs of others. Their willingness to help and their supportive nature makes them an asset to any relationship. Oranges are careful to maintain a courteous, polite, and restrained demeanor and will do whatever it takes to create conflict-free environments.

2. Social. They'd rather be with people than be alone. Oranges are very social and enjoy spending time with those they care about. An Orange's idea of a good time is being involved in activities where people can enjoy each other's company, learn more about each other's needs, and share in the bonds of fellowship. Whether it's a quiet dinner party for close friends or a major event, an Orange will see to it that everyone is comfortable and made to feel special.

3. Generous. The Oranges' generosity and sensitivity are their greatest contributions to other personality colors. They give their time and resources. Oranges aren't the type of people who'll wait to be asked for assistance; they'll just jump in. Their generous nature motivates them to lend a helping hand to anyone who needs it, whether it's family, friends, or even total strangers. Oranges would give someone the shirt off their back if they felt it could help. However, they would expect acknowledgment and appreciation in return.

4. Caring. Oranges are genuinely concerned about people and their emotional well-being. They're thoughtful, considerate, and act from the heart. They understand the need to have someone who truly cares and someone you can count on, so they show their affection with sincere actions and outreach. Since their innermost desire is to be of service to humankind, they're interested in seeing that people are treated with respect and dignity. They want to ensure that everyone is appreciated for their uniqueness and contributions.

5. Emotional. Emotions rule the Oranges' lives and drive their behavior. They're so sensitive that it's easy for them to get their feelings hurt over the slightest things. They can actually sense when others are hurting, struggling, or feeling insecure. This can be a double-edged sword: On the one hand, it helps them take an emotional pulse to find out what's really going on around them; but on the other, it distresses them to see others suffer.

6. Traditional. Oranges are traditionalists and are unwavering in their perceptions of what a love relationship should be like. They're reliable, loyal, devoted, and dependable, and expect their mate to be the same. They believe that gender roles are important and that responsibilities should be shared. Other personality colors look to Oranges for security and stability. They know that an Orange will always provide an organized and conflict-free environment and will give them the support and compassion that lets them know they're loved and appreciated.

7. Apprehensive. Oranges fret, worry, and are continually apprehensive. They seem to always be looking over their shoulder when things are going well, as if waiting for the other shoe to drop. They worry about anything and everything, and consequently live with the ongoing anxiety that something bad is going to happen. Oranges don't like surprises, so they use their apprehension to help them stay alert and feel in control of their lives. When they're anxious, they're second-guessing themselves and fretting about things they have no control over.

8. Moody. Oranges are moody. They think that life is either good or it's bad. They're either happy or sad, optimistic or depressed. When Oranges are cheerful, everything is wonderful and their outlook on life is positive. When they're down, everything is a problem, and they're very difficult to be around. Their mood swings are directly connected to how they're feeling about their relationship and whether they believe others are appreciating them or not.

9. Devoted. Oranges are devoted, loyal, and steadfast. Their dedication to their relationship is so strong that they'll stand by their mate through thick and thin—no matter what happens. Because of their commitment, it isn't uncommon for an Orange to endure both emotional and physical discomfort if they believe that it will help those they love.

10. Guilt-ridden. The burden of guilt weighs heavily on the Orange's shoulders, so it's difficult for them to make demands on other people, because they worry that they'll put someone in a position of having to do something unpleasant. They feel bad when they do something wrong, buy something expensive, or believe they've hurt anyone's feelings. Oranges see it as their responsibility to be peacemakers, creating an environment where everyone can get along. When they're unable to do so, they feel guilty and believe they've let people down.

What Love Means to an Orange

Oranges are traditional and sentimental when it comes to love. They see it as being selfless and requiring both people to put the needs of the other person before their own. As a matter of fact, it's incomprehensible to Oranges that anyone would even think about not doing that when they're in love. Their only focus is on the *we* part of the relationship and working together as a couple, not on the *me* part. They see *me* behavior as being selfish, insensitive, and a detriment to the quality of their union. They believe that love creates a place in the heart where two people can meet and care for each other, building a strong emotional connection where the needs of the couple are far more important than those of the individual.

Love, for the Orange, means being responsive to their mate's needs and seeing that they're met. This can sometimes be frustrating, since it may mean putting their own life on hold while supporting and taking care of their partner. Yet, from the Orange's perspective, it's worth it, because in return they get the love, security, and stability they need in order to feel good about their relationship. Oranges express their affection through all the things they do, such as helping out whenever they can, running errands, cooking, picking up the children, shopping, doing laundry, and anything else their mate doesn't want (or have time) to do. They use these actions as criteria for determining how well they're caring for those they love, and they use their mate's expression of appreciation as a way of feeling loved.

Oranges see love as a deep emotional bond between two people that forms a commitment so strong that it can withstand the ups and downs that all relationships experience over the course of time. They believe that love should be supportive, safe, comforting, and predictable. Oranges want permanence—they don't want to invest time or energy if they feel that the connection may not endure. They're only interested if there's mutual admiration and the objective is to create a long-term commitment. Consequently, they're very particular about who they date. If they decide that someone would be a good provider, mate, and parent, then they're willing to invest the time cultivating that connection. Having a family is very important to Oranges, so don't be surprised if they want to start one very early on in the relationship.

Being loved offers Oranges the emotional constancy they need to cope with the challenges of life. Giving affection is what they live for and provides them with a sense of belonging. They see love as a verb, meaning that it requires being actively involved in the process and demands constant attention. They don't take it for granted, nor do they assume that it will just continue to grow and flourish without some help. Oranges work hard at keeping their relationships together and will tend to overlook behavior that puts it in jeopardy. They're dedicated, faithful, and committed, and expect their mate to act the same way.

Doing things together is important to Oranges, and they enjoy sharing interests and activities. They're careful to promote harmony, and work hard to create a loving environment. These personality types bring a lot of expectations into their relationship. They expect their mate to be there for them when they're needed, to be as committed as they are to making things work, and to be sensitive to their emotional needs. When these expectations aren't met, Oranges become dismayed and distressed and withdraw emotionally. They want cooperation and teamwork and will become resentful if those they love aren't doing their fair share. They expect mutual respect and commitment.

The Orange's Expression of Love's Many Splendors

Romance

When it comes to romance, the more sentimental the gesture, the better Oranges like it. As with everything else, they're traditionalists, so they'll use special occasions—including anniversaries, birthdays, Easter, Mother's Day, Father's Day, Christmas, Hanukah, Halloween, and Valentine's Day—to do all the sweet things that say "I love you." They enjoy acting from the heart and being thoughtful in ways that send the message loud and clear how deeply they care for their mate. It's important to them that their partner doesn't have to wonder whether they're loved or not. Oranges see romance as another way to create the emotional intimacy they desire and need, so they'll use it as a means of ensuring that their bonds remain strong. It keeps the relationship playful and shows their devotion.

Oranges see the communication process as being an integral part of romance because it creates the opportunity to share feelings. However, because of the demands of life, spending time just sitting around and talking isn't always easy, so Oranges will create a romantic getaway where they and their mate can spend quality time together. They can share their emotions, activities, and interests; make love without external distractions; avoid the pressures of a schedule; lie in bed without feeling guilty; and do whatever they want, whenever they want. Anything that makes it possible for them to talk about important subjects is the Orange's idea of a wonderfully romantic time.

Oranges do enjoy the finer things in life, even though they won't ask for them, so they expect their mate to romantically indulge them once in a while by doing something extravagant. This can be anything from buying a lavish gift or going on an expensive vacation, to taking them to an upscale restaurant on a special occasion. However, when it comes to a nice dinner out, Oranges aren't interested in going to a place where the objective is simply to fill the belly. They're interested in going somewhere that will fill the heart. Romantic gestures for the Orange should be sensual pleasures; they'll want to do things and go places where the ambiance stirs them emotionally, getting them in the mood and fueling the fire of passion.

The Orange female loves receiving expensive gifts because they show other people that she's very special to someone and obviously in a relationship where she's appreciated. While a simple "I love you" shows her affection in private, a nice piece of jewelry, a new car, and other costly trinkets tell other people how much she's loved. In some parts of the world, when a man seeks the hand of a woman, he must go to her father and not only ask for permission, but must show through gifts just how much value he places on her. One such culture uses cows because of their sacred value. The common gift ranges from one to several cows, so when a suitor offers the father 100 cows for the hand of his daughter, he's not only telling the father that she's valued, he's letting the community know it, too. Every Orange female would like to be seen as a 100-cow woman.

Passion

As with romance, passion is intended to deepen the emotional bond Oranges have with their mate and give them the warm fuzzies they need in order to feel loved. Passion, for the Orange, doesn't necessarily lead to sex. This splendor is merely another way of showing how deeply they care and an expression of their desire for togetherness. Oranges see passionate foreplay as another way to merge hearts, and it's an important contributor to the quality of their relationship.

Both male and female Oranges can't seem to turn on their passion switch at the drop of a hat or just because their mate is aroused. They need time to prepare themselves emotionally and get in the mood. They see passion as part of the seduction process and expect their mate to be patient and not try to hurry them. They enjoy engaging in activities that give their mate pleasure, while at the same time fulfilling them emotionally, such as dressing in something seductive and watching sensual movies and love stories. They may be turned off by pornography or activities where they feel that a person is being exploited or abused.

Even spending quiet one-on-one quality time is part of the expression of passion for an Orange. Since they equate this splendor with sensitivity, seduction, and caring, they enjoy its more subdued aspects that convey tenderness and deep affection. Expressions that are blatant, forthright, raw, overly aggressive, and what they consider crude are turnoffs. These suggest that their mate is more interested in their body than in them as a person. Should Oranges find themself in a relationship where the only objective for being passionate is sex, their desire for it will quickly fade, and it could even turn into something they dislike and dread.

Intimacy

Oranges need, crave, and yearn for intimacy because it's the sole measurement they use to determine the quality of their relationship. It tells them that they're okay, loved, and appreciated. It makes all they do for those they love worthwhile and is the ultimate expression of caring. Intimacy represents a deep sense of connectedness and is the glue that holds a relationship together, even when the demands of life try to tear it apart. However, the only expression of this quality that Oranges place real value on is emotional intimacy.

If we were to ask an Orange to prioritize the four expressions of intimacy and rank their importance, this what we'd see: (1) emotional, (2) physical, (3) mental, and (4) spiritual. As far as they're concerned, the first type is the only one that deepens the bonds of love and offers the closeness they need and require. It alone will transform the insecurities they feel inside and feed the innermost longings of their heart.

The bond created by emotional intimacy reinforces how they feel about their mate and solidifies their desire to remain committed to the relationship. It allows them to express their appreciation in a way that's thoughtful and sensitive, opening up the lines of communication so that they can safely and confidently express their emotional vulnerabilities and fears.

At the same time, the emotional bond makes it possible for their mate to do the same. Oranges need to know their partner's vulnerabilities so that they can better understand how to provide the support needed to keep them from growing apart. Emotional intimacy represents a promise to each other to make things work. It forms the foundation upon which a long-term relationship can be built.

Sex

Oranges see sex as another expression of emotional intimacy and a way of deepening the commitment with their mate. They prefer to refer to it as "lovemaking" because "sex" sounds so unemotional and insensitive. When they're in the mood, Oranges thoroughly enjoy the sharing of physical pleasures and getting in touch with the sensations of their body. It makes them feel appreciated, accepted, complete, and emotionally satisfied. It helps them manage their feelings of inadequacy, and contributes to their overall emotional well-being. Oranges savor the expressions of tenderness and caring that come with lovemaking and use those expressions to influence both their excitement and the pleasure they get from it.

Oranges, both male and female, are moody when it comes to sex because their desire is directly tied to where they are emotionally, especially the emotional state of their relationship. If they're experiencing tension or there have been hurtful words exchanged, their interest in sex quickly diminishes to the point that they not only don't want to go to bed with their mate, they don't even want to be in the same room with them. Since Oranges are so strongly influenced by their emotions, anything that distresses them causes them to lose interest. The "I have a headache" cliché sends the message loud and clear: They're not interested, so leave them alone.

If their mate tries to guilt or coerce them into having sex, Oranges will become resentful, and their mate runs the risk of turning what should be a pleasurable experience into something that's an unpleasant and perfunctory obligation. Oranges are also known to withhold sex as a means of expressing their displeasure when their mate has hurt their feelings or been insensitive toward them. If the issue isn't resolved in a timely manner, it can lead to lengthy periods of abstinence, until their mate apologizes or does something to demonstrate that they're sorry.

Communication

Out of all the splendors of love, communication ranks highest on the list to the Orange personality. From their perspective, it's imperative to keep the lines open if the relationship is to grow and flourish. Oranges need to share how and what they're feeling, and become disgusted and dismayed when their mate ignores their emotions or acts disinterested in what they have to say. For Oranges, this is another integral part in the emotional-bonding process and is an essential component of intimacy.

Oranges believe that this process should include both talking and listening, which means their mate had better engage in both. They expect their partner to open up to them and share their feelings, as well as be an active, sympathetic listener, just like they are. When Oranges have something important to say or want to discuss their emotions, they expect their mate to stop what they're doing and listen. They don't want them off in a fog thinking about what they're going to say next or jumping in and interrupting before they have time to get things off their chest.

Oranges need to be able to discuss all emotions, including both the positive and negative ones. They want to be heard and be taken seriously; they don't want to have their feelings dismissed or have what they're saying chalked up to just being emotional. Should their mate dare to do either, the Orange will become incensed and outraged and will cut them off sexually. The absolutely worst thing their mate can do is to ignore or silence them by saying that they aren't interested in how the Orange is feeling.

Without quality one-on-one time to talk and being able to share how they feel, Oranges feel distant, disconnected, and even isolated from their mate. They find it difficult to stay emotionally engaged and maintain the closeness they need in order to feel loved. If tension and conflict are ever going to surface in their relationship, it will be when the lines of communication break down.

Oranges use words that elicit an emotional reaction and tend to ask "why" questions. By doing so, they're able to get a sense of how someone feels about something. Oranges aren't interested in superfluous or superficial conversations; they want to get right to the heart of the matter and find out what's going on deep inside. They want to know what a person is afraid of and why.

Oranges see the communication process as creating an intimate environment where a person can safely and comfortably share their fears and vulnerabilities. They feel that by encouraging these kinds of conversations, there's less chance that they'll be caught off guard emotionally. Since their nature is to worry about what people think of them, and to live in a constant state of low-grade anxiety, it's important for Oranges to be kept in the emotional loop conversationally. This makes it easier for them to manage their worrying, and it alleviates many of the anxieties they feel.

An ongoing issue for Oranges is that they continually feel misunderstood. This baffles them because they perceive themselves as good communicators. And yes, they are effective in telling others how they're feeling, but when it comes to asking for what they need physically and emotionally, they tend to miss the mark. Oranges don't believe they should have to ask for love; they just expect their mate to know how much they need it. When an Orange finally does have to request something that seems obvious—such as asking their mate to say "I love you"—it disappoints them and undermines their relationship. It causes them to see their mate as being insensitive, selfish, egocentric, unconcerned about them, and only interested in meeting their own needs. Having to ask for care and love makes the Orange feel taken advantage of, emotionally vulnerable, and needy. It breaks down the lines of communication and makes them rethink opening up their heart to anyone.

Commitment

The desire for a lifelong commitment is perhaps the greatest gift an Orange brings into their relationships. They place a tremendous value on it, viewing it as a sacred union between two people, which provides the foundation upon which a stable and secure long-term relationship can be built. Commitment, for an Orange, represents giving their mate their love and heart and trusting them implicitly with both. In return, they need someone they can trust, so they can relax and enjoy the benefits that come from sharing their life. Oranges dedicate themselves forever, till death do us part, and living happily ever after. Anything less isn't acceptable to them. Consequently, they're steadfast in doing things that create permanence and ensure that the flames of love will continue to burn brightly.

Since Oranges have such a strong need for a relationship, it isn't uncommon for them to stay in situations that are abusive or find themselves with a mate who's domineering and overly controlling. When I've asked Oranges why they do this, many have said that they stay because they'd rather be in a bad relationship than be without one. They have a tremendous fear of abandonment. Besides, the Orange believes that they'll be able to change their mate over the course of time if they just continue to love them and see that their needs are met.

Another reason the Oranges stay in less-than-desirable relationships is because they're afraid of conflict and don't want to be responsible for hurting their mate's feelings. Consequently, they'll make excuses for why they aren't leaving. They'll say things such as, "Oh, they're just having a bad day," or "The pressures of their job are really getting to them," or "I'm okay and need to stay while we work things out," or "They need me—I don't know how they'd get along if I were to leave."

Taking on the role of a martyr is something the Orange does comfortably, especially if they perceive that it will keep the relationship intact. However, should their commitment of love be betrayed, they aren't quick to forgive or forget how much they've been hurt. And if their mate isn't remorseful, these kind, sensitive, caring, and loving personalities will become spiteful, vengeful, bitter, and maybe even nasty.

How Love Changes with Age

As those with this personality type age, they become more secure in themselves and more comfortable with their relationship. They settle down emotionally and are less reactive and emotionally volatile. There's less of a tendency to be a martyr as they soften and become more objective. Their rigidity about what's acceptable and what's not subsides, as do their expectations of others. They're more open and receptive to change and find themselves wanting more excitement in their lives and less responsibility for others.

In their 30s, the demands of life and family change their perception of love and find them having very little time to enjoy the pleasures of spending time with their mate. However, in their late 30s, Oranges begin to find their voice and become more assertive in asking for what they need and want. They're less willing to shove things under the rug or dismiss insensitive behavior just because someone is having a bad day. They become less submissive and concerned with keeping the peace. They'll express their resentment when they feel that they're being taken advantage of, and will tell their mate if they're not feeling appreciated. This isn't meant to imply that they're less caring or less sensitive to the needs of those they love—it's just that their tolerance to remain silent and suppress things diminishes, as does their willingness to put their needs on the back burner.

In their 40s, the Orange finally begins to feel that they can start doing things for themselves and for their reasons. At this age, they find themselves in an interesting place in life, because the needs of the family and the responsibilities that come with caring for others are no longer what drives them or dictates what they do. They realize that they're needed less and find themselves with more time on their hands. This means that they can finally pursue the activities, interests, and hobbies they've wanted to try and become more involved in doing things outside their relationship.

While this can be an exciting and liberating time for the Orange, it can also be threatening for their mate, because suddenly their needs aren't the most important thing to the Orange, and they aren't the center of attention. At this stage in life, the Orange begins to pass on some of the responsibilities to their mate, whose life is then going to change. If there ever was a time in this relationship where conflict is going to arise or there's the potential for the relationship to end, it's at this stage.

By the time the Orange reaches their 50s, their skin is thicker and they're less apt to back down from a confrontational situation. Instead of always feeling guilty, they'll turn things around and make their mate feel bad. The Orange will point out aggressively how they've had to always put the needs of others before their own, and they're tired of taking a backseat. At this stage in life, the Orange is more interested in developing a mutually satisfying relationship where they can enjoy their mate and spend quality time with them, rather than perpetuating old patterns that are limiting and restrictive. In their 50s, Oranges are ready to fall in love all over again, once more finding the romance and passion they crave.

Orange's Fears, Insecurities, and Anxieties

The prime motivator behind everything an Orange does is to take care of other people, so a safe, secure, and loving relationship is paramount to their sense of well-being. Without such a union, they're emotionally incomplete, and it's difficult for them to feel good about themselves. Consequently, many of the fears, insecurities, and anxieties that they experience center around their relationship and their interaction with their mate. There isn't any other personality color who's as greatly affected by what others think of them, or that has such a high need to please people, as an Orange. Here are some of the emotional issues that they constantly deal with:

- Fear of abandonment

- Fear of being without a relationship and emotionally unsupported

- Feelings of vulnerability because they think that they don't have any say in what will happen to them

- Fear of being emotionally manipulated and controlled by other people

- Feelings of resentment over the sexual authority of their mate (or the opposite sex in general)

- Anxiety that they're not good enough

- Fear of doing something wrong

- Insecurities about being victimized because of sex, ethnic origin, or sexual preference

- Anxiety about change and fear of the unknown

- Feelings of inadequacy

- Low self-worth

- Fear of being emotionally vulnerable and needy

- Lack of emotional intimacy

The Evolutionary Stage of a Relationship That Oranges Are Most Attracted To

The stage that's most appealing to the Orange is commitment, because it's there that they can stop worrying about being alone and begin feeling secure in knowing that they're a part of a long-term relationship. This stage also indicates that they've finally found a person who will love them, care for them, fulfill their emotional needs, and be a good mate and parent. It alleviates their fears about not being worthy of having a relationship and tells other people that the Orange is okay and there's no longer a need to worry about them.

When it comes to consecrating their commitment, Oranges are conventional and believe in the sanctity of marriage. They want everyone who's important to them to share in their rites of commitment, so they'll tend to plan a traditional ceremony of some kind, surrounded by the people who love them. They want their families and friends to feel comfortable with their decision and share in their happiness. They long for others to see that they're not entering into the relationship lightly, but instead are willing to spend the rest of their life with someone they trust.

The Evolutionary Stage of a Relationship That's the Most Difficult for an Orange

When I've asked Oranges which stage they felt was the most difficult for them, they've said dating, because there are so many unknowns. They didn't know whether the relationship would last, if they might do something wrong to destroy the connection, whether they could give their date what they wanted, or even if they'd be accepted for who they are. Their general consensus was that this stage left them feeling the most emotionally vulnerable and uneasy. They also felt that this is where most of the games were played and the element of being untruthful was at its highest. For them, dating felt more like a masquerade party than a search to find true love. They complained that it was emotionally tiring and draining, and found it difficult to see through the many masks people use to hide their feelings.

Oranges told me that they'd use this stage to establish the criteria for deciding what they wanted in a mate, and as a means of measuring whether the person could live up to their expectations. It wasn't unusual for them to size up their date within the first few minutes of conversation by counting up the number of times the person used the words *I* or *me*. They relied on their first impressions to tell them whether a person was in contention for their affections or should be dropped off the A-list. The Oranges, for the most part, weren't interested in expending either time or energy on someone who was so self-focused that they weren't even interested in reciprocating in the conversation or in learning more about them.

I asked Oranges what qualities they looked for when dating to determine if a person would make a good mate. Here are some of the things they felt were important:

- Sensitivity
- Caring for others
- Thoughtfulness
- Punctuality
- Financial security
- Self-confidence
- Having common interests
- Being physically attractive

- Having a close relationship with their family
- Wanting a family of their own
- Being willing to spend the money and effort needed to win their hearts
- The ability to express appreciation
- An interest in hearing how they feel about things
- Viewing sex as more than just a biological release

From what I was told, they use the rule "Three strikes and you're out" as their means of determining whether they'd invest more time and energy in a person. If a person doesn't measure up in three of the qualities listed, they're out of the game.

Overview of the Orange Personality	
Basic needs:	• Be in a relationship that's conflict free and that promotes harmony • A supportive relationship • Feel appreciated for what they give and all they do • Financial security and stability
Emotional needs:	• Open lines of communication so that they can share their emotions • Unwavering commitment and emotional sensitivity • Shared interests and doing things together • Fidelity
Key strengths:	• Loyal, devoted, and sensitive • Considerate, cooperative, and understanding • Generous with time and resources • Faithful
Key weaknesses:	• Inability to ask for what they need • Emotionally vulnerable and needy • Emotionally explosive and unpre-dictable • Unable to deal with sudden changes and surprises

Overview of the Orange Personality, cont'd.	
Primary fear:	• Fear of abandonment
Attracted to people who are:	• Financially secure and stable • Interested in a family • Physically attractive • Confident and aggressive
Dislike people who are:	• Wishy-washy and indecisive • Opinionated and overconfident • Unorganized, lazy, and not punctual
Relationship expectations:	• Mutual support and commitment
Value in a relationship:	• Thoughtful, sensitive, and caring gestures that show how much they're appreciated
Room for improvement:	• Learning to ask for what they need • Managing their emotional volatility • Becoming less rigid in their expectations of those they love
Annoyances:	• Being taken for granted and having their good nature abused
Causes of stress:	• Sudden changes and surprises • Overloaded schedules
Relationship challenge:	• Learning to let go of the perception that their relationship defines who they are

Hot Tips for Dealing with Oranges	
Love	Remember to say "Thank you," and share expressions that let them know you're sensitive to their emotional needs.
Romance	Surprise them with things they enjoy and that show you care and are thinking about them.
Passion	If you want to get them in the mood, plan a date night where the two of you can enjoy each other's company and turn the evening into a sensual and sexual experience.
Sex	Go slow and be patient until they take the initiative. Then lie back and enjoy their eager desire to give you pleasure.
Communication	Actively listen to what they have to say and sincerely acknowledge how they're feeling.

Helpful Hints for Oranges in Dealing with Other Personality Colors	
Love	Learn to accept praise and appreciation and value it in the light in which it's offered.
Romance	Create special occasions and opportunities to rekindle your love and keep the flames of passion burning brightly.
Passion	Ask your partner what turns them on and what you can do to heighten their enjoyment of intimacy.
Sex	If you aren't in the mood, express it. Don't turn making love into an obligation or something that you resent.
Communication	If you're feeling ignored or silenced, express it to them before it becomes an emotional issue for you.

CHAPTER SEVEN

The Yellow Personality:
The "Let's-Do-It-Differently" People

Janet has always felt like a square peg trying to fit into a round world. As long as she can remember, she hasn't been the stereotypical female. To begin with, she's logical and analytical rather than emotional and nurturing. Next, she was never interested in playing with dolls, but preferred taking things apart and figuring out how to understand them or make them better. She chose to spend time fishing and hunting rather than hanging out with girlfriends. And when her friends were going to dances, she was taking auto shop and spending time working on her car.

She's always been ambitious, with an insatiable desire to learn, and admits that she's her own worst enemy because she's always pushing herself to be better. She says that she's never satisfied with what she does or what she accomplishes and tends to continually escalate the expectations she has of herself. She admits to being a perfectionist and says that it's important to be her own person rather than trying to conform with what other people expect of her.

She understands how her need to be perfect is both motivating and limiting. On the one hand, it pushes her to step outside her comfort zones and prevents complacency. On the other, she spends an exorbitant amount of time analyzing before she can act—"analysis paralysis." She sees taking the time to think things through as more important than making an impulsive decision, yet even knowing this, she still becomes frustrated when she doesn't act quickly enough.

Janet loves to solve problems—the more complex, the better. She says that she has a compulsive need to jump into any conversation or situation whenever a problem surfaces or is identified, even if her input isn't wanted or asked for. I asked her to explain what she meant, and she told me about a lunch with some friends. As they were talking, all she heard were problems. She said that when one of them finally took a breath, she proceeded to jump in and offer some ideas and suggestions as to how to solve things.

The moment she did, her friend looked at her with a puzzled expression and asked, "What problem? I don't have a problem. I was just talking." Janet responded, "If there wasn't a problem, why did you make it sound as if there were?" Then her friends proceeded to tease her about always looking for trouble just so she could offer solutions.

When I asked Janet about her relationships, she said that she didn't have very many that she would consider meaningful. Instead, most of her friends were business associates and people interested in her work. She found that it was necessary to keep some distance from them in order to protect her privacy. She told me of one personal relationship she had and why it didn't work: She needs the freedom to do what she wants and isn't at all interested in losing her independence and autonomy, even for love. Janet said that if she could find a mate who was more of a partner and who understood her needs, then she might be interested in giving it another try. Then she quickly added that she wasn't necessarily looking for a relationship because she enjoyed living alone.

A General Description of the Yellow Personality

A Yellow's greatest asset is their mind. They're independent thinkers who pride themselves on being able to utilize and integrate both their logic and imagination to come up with creative solutions. They're visionaries and get great pleasure in creating innovative ways to do things differently and make things better. It doesn't matter to a Yellow if it's never been done before or if it didn't work; they're confident that if they can conceive it, they can achieve it. They know very well that if all else fails, they can fall back on their resourcefulness and determination.

Yellows pride themselves on their intellectual skills, inventiveness, and ability to create original thoughts. Consequently, they tend to be involved in the cutting edge of technology and the design and creation of new products. They're intense people and passionate dreamers who become singularly focused once they set their mind on something that intrigues or interests them. They're deep thinkers and encourage others to think outside of the box and to ask "What if" questions.

A Yellow's greatest contribution to their mate and their relationship is the ability to solve problems, especially when no solutions are obvious. They're masterful at using their minds to create alternative solutions when no one else seems to be able to come up with any. Their need to problem-solve is driven more by not wanting to be caught off guard, appear unprepared, or get blindsided than by anything else. Consequently, they're what I refer to as "preventive problem solvers," meaning that they anticipate future issues and start creating solutions before trouble ever arises.

It isn't uncommon for Yellows to play out scenarios in their mind contemplating what they'll do in a given situation, to hold internal conversations preparing for what they'll say should those scenarios take place, or to create a variety of solutions anticipating the unexpected. Their credo is the same as the Boy Scout motto: "Be Prepared."

Yellows want to be identified as being part of the solution, so they have very little tolerance for those who deal only in problems. It's incomprehensible to them that people won't help themselves, and that they'd choose to stick with what's tried-and-true but may not work, rather than attempting something different. The problem is that Yellows fail to remember that not every personality color is as solution driven as they are.

The best word to describe the Yellow personality is *self*. They're *self-starters, self-assured, self-confident, self-reliant, self-motivated,* and *self-made*. Their sense of self is so strong that they don't believe they need other people—nor do they want other people telling them what to do or how to do it. In fact, it really irritates them when someone takes it upon him- or herself to try to direct their activities. Should you ever find yourself in this kind of situation, don't be surprised if they become sarcastic, tactless, and emotionally cutting in their strong verbal reactions.

Yellows want the freedom to think for themselves and use their intellectual capabilities to expand their intelligence through the pursuit of both knowledge and wisdom. Because of their logical nature, they aren't emotional and don't have the need to express how they're feeling. They're very private and keep to themselves, which can make it difficult to know where you stand with them, "read" them, or live with them. However, this doesn't mean that they're not sensitive, because they are—and they're prone to getting their feelings hurt easily. They just believe that it's better to keep all of that buried inside rather than inviting someone to use those feelings against them in a conflict situation. The only time a Yellow will open up emotionally is if they feel that they can fully trust the person implicitly.

Yellows are never content with the status quo or following someone else's directions. They see rules as being made for people who aren't willing to make their own. Consequently, they're seen as nonconformists, mavericks, and poor team players. In many ways this is true, because they have a natural aversion to following others' lead. They're not interested in taking the path of least resistance. Yellows want to do things their way, even if it means challenging the system and those who are in authority. Their unwillingness to conform makes them difficult to control—and difficult to be in a relationship with. They aren't willing to play the game just to be liked, or for that matter, to be loved.

It's important for a Yellow to be their own person and feel in control of their own destiny. They're not willing to put their fate in another person's hands, even if that person is their mate. They want to be the captain of their own ship and will challenge anyone who tries to put them in a subordinate role. These self-reliant personalities are perfectly content to be alone; they don't need someone just for the sake of being part of a couple.

When a Yellow does decide to enter into a relationship, they'll look for an equal partner, someone who will complement their strengths, respecting and accepting them for who they are. Yellows aren't interested in anyone who will require that they change their identity or lose any part of themselves. They want a union that supports individuality and gives both people room to grow personally and professionally.

By nature, Yellows are skeptical and suspicious of people and their motives, so they approach relationships cautiously and with some trepidation. They want to be sure that the other person can be trusted before they become romantically involved. They're keen observers and are quick to recognize when a person's words and actions don't match. And most important, they're not interested in people who don't share the same principles or place the same value on integrity that they do.

Yellows are private, reserved people who aren't inclined to entrust others with their feelings. They avoid lengthy conversations that involve displaying sentiment or expressing emotions. Their reserved, aloof nature makes it easy for them to remain detached from situations and people so that they can observe from an arm's-length, nonemotional perspective.

The Yellow personality tends to create a faux persona so that others won't discover their idiosyncrasies and vulnerabilities, which they believe could (and would) be used against them. This mask helps keep people at a distance and serves as a form of self-protection. Consequently, other personalities see them as being hard to get to know, standoffish, cold, evasive, and noncommittal—which is exactly the way Yellows prefer to be perceived.

Ten Observable Behavioral Traits of a Yellow Personality

Here are ten of the most observable behavioral traits of the Yellow personality. Each quality contributes to their natural leadership skills and their ability to be such effective problem solvers. Although other personality colors may display similar behavior, a person who is a Yellow will demonstrate them more consistently and frequently.

1. Ambitious. Yellows believe in setting high standards for themselves. They're objective driven and goal oriented. They're determined, intense, tenacious, and singularly focused when it comes to seeing that their goals are met. Yellows are motivated by achievement and aren't timid about displaying their ambitious nature. They seek to excel in anything they do and strive to out-perform other people.

2. Honorable. Yellows place great value on integrity. They have very high ethical standards, which they use as the basis for self-conduct. They're fair, honest, trustworthy, truthful, and unwavering in their commitment. If other people challenge the Yellow's intentions or integrity, they'll become verbally aggressive and openly confrontational. It helps to remember that it's okay to question their decisions, but never doubt their integrity.

3. Self-confident. Yellows believe in themselves and are confident in their abilities. They're not timid or meek, nor do they give in to intimidation or succumb to their anxieties. Instead, they'll muster up the courage needed to face their fears and will move forward with confidence and determination. Yellows have an inner knowing that their purpose in life is to make a difference, and it's their self-confidence that makes it possible.

4. Tenacious. *Impossible* isn't a word Yellows relate to, especially when it comes to finding a better way to do something. When Yellows want something and set their minds to getting it, it's best to stay out of their way, because their tenacious nature makes them a formidable force. They seem to make things happen even when other people believe they can't be done.

5. Visionary. Creative thinking and their ability to go beyond the norm make Yellows masterful visionaries. They're able to anticipate the needs of the future and create innovative solutions. The most challenging words to the Yellow are "It can't be done," because that assertion excites their imagination and stimulates their minds. They're always looking for ways to do things differently and better.

6. Skeptical. Yellows tend to be suspicious, and their inherent nature is not to trust people. They'll usually take a wait-and-see position until they're sure someone is who they claim to be and can determine if they're trustworthy. Yellows are quick to size a person up, and they rely on their first impressions to decide whether they'd be interested in developing a relationship with someone. If the initial meeting is favorable, they're more inclined to take the next step. If it isn't, they'll withdraw and avoid any kind of interaction.

7. Reserved. Yellows are reserved people and use their standoffish, aloof demeanor as a means of protecting themselves. Their arrogance makes them difficult to be around and even more difficult to get to know. People see them as unapproachable, egotistical, and complex. This works fine for the Yellow, because it keeps other people—including their mate—from discovering their insecurities and vulnerabilities.

8. Cerebral. Yellows are deep thinkers and spend a lot of time in their head. They see their mental acuity as being their most valuable asset. They believe that people should continually seek to expand their consciousness and their desire to learn and create original thought. Those who are mentally lazy and won't think for themselves aren't the kind of people this personality will hang out with.

9. Fiercely independent. Yellows need autonomy and the freedom to do things their own way. They don't want others telling them what to do or how to do it. They'll rarely seek outside opinions or advice, because they want to draw their own conclusions and march to their own drummer. They won't allow others to control them and aren't interested in being in any relationship that requires their being accountable to someone else.

10. Nonconformist. Yellows want to appear to be different, so they'll resist following what's tried-and-true. Their defiant nature motivates them to write their own rules rather than following societal norms. They aren't easily intimidated into doing things they don't want to, and they aren't willing to forego their individuality to comply with the desires of others. They regard themselves as extraordinary and enjoy coloring outside the lines.

What Love Means to a Yellow

As with everything else about a Yellow, they tend to be independent thinkers even when it comes to defining what love means to them. When I queried the Yellows about what love means to them, you'd have thought I'd asked them to solve a potentially impossible problem. They were excited by the prospect, challenged by the concept, and immobilized by the fear that they might not get the answer right. I assured them that as a fellow Yellow, I wasn't trying to trick them, nor was I looking for a "right" answer. I merely wanted to find out what love meant to *them* and how *they'd* define it.

Most Yellows said that they'd have to think about it and get back to me, because it was a complex question and certainly didn't have just one answer. Some even admitted that they were reluctant to share their definition because it was so different from what society says it should be. Part of the reason for all of the disclaimers is that Yellows pride themselves on their originality and being nontraditional, and their perception of this emotion is no exception.

Yellows define love as being global, meaning that there are different kinds and degrees. They see it as having a variety of connotations, connections, and expressions—and one kind doesn't fit all as we've been led to believe. Yellows see the traditional ideas of love as being limiting, boring, stifling, restrictive, and lacking ingenuity and imagination. Instead, they see it as being exciting, stimulating, engaging, expansive, and mutually fulfilling.

Love, for Yellows, is a state of mind, and how they participate in its splendors is solely dependent upon where they are mentally. If their mind is clear, they'll connect mentally with their mate and experience strong feelings of passion. They'll freely express their needs and desires and enjoy the pleasures of love. On the other hand, when they're mentally preoccupied, it's as if those feelings don't exist. The degrees of affection that a Yellow feels vary from hot to cold, so they know that if they're going to keep love alive, it will require them to stay mentally involved in making the relationship work. Yellows take commitment seriously and don't enter into it lightly. They understand that it requires attention and mindfulness.

Yellows describe being in love as a partnership where both people have an equal amount invested in making it succeed, and the same amount of say in how it should work. Yellows are very selective about whom they choose for their partner and are only interested in someone they respect, and whom they perceive as being an intellectual peer. They want a partner who has similar interests, values, and principles, and who also has a high degree of integrity. They're looking for someone who's independent, resourceful, and self-reliant—not needy or unwilling to accept responsibility for their own actions.

Their mate will be strong enough to stand up for themselves and emotionally self-sufficient, yet also accepting enough to put up with their idiosyncrasies and nonconformist attitude. They have no interest in emotionally complex or volatile relationships, or in anyone who's emotionally high maintenance, either in time or energy. Yellows are well aware of the fact that calming others down isn't something they're good at, and they don't want to be stuck doing that for the rest of their lives.

Yellows aren't inclined to get swept away in a flood of feelings as some of the other personality colors are, especially in the initial stages of falling in love, nor do they find it necessary to express their devotion in words. Unfortunately, their lack of verbal expressions is often misconstrued as not caring or being insensitive, neither of which is true. They just assume that their partner knows they're cherished, so saying "I love you" isn't something they think about or see as necessary. In fact, they believe that saying it too much or too often minimizes its significance and lessens its value.

While this approach works well for Yellows, it can be frustrating and hurtful to someone who needs emotional reassurance and who wants to hear declarations of love frequently. Instead of using words to show how much they care, Yellows express themselves through the little things they do, which are meaningful and thoughtful acts that they personally value. They also display their affection through their strong sense of responsibility and need to protect those they care about.

The opposite of love isn't hate, it's indifference, and the Yellow personality is capable of going to indifference very quickly. What causes them to reach this point in their relationship is somewhat of a mystery. However, here are several of the triggers that the Yellows shared:

- They think they're being taken advantage of.
- They lose respect for their partner.
- Their partner isn't willing to accept responsibility for their actions.
- Their partner's judgment is flawed.
- Their partner isn't truthful.
- Their partner isn't trustworthy.

Yellows have high expectations when it comes to love and how they think their partner should contribute to the relationship. They can be judgmental and critical and will apply their own standards to how the other person should act. They don't have any patience or tolerance for someone who lies or is lazy. If Yellows sense that their relationship isn't going anywhere and love has lost its challenge, they'll emotionally detach and distance themselves. This alone creates a tremendous amount of stress for their mate, because it's as if one moment the Yellow is deeply in love and involved with them, and the next moment they're cold, indifferent, and emotionally detached.

However, even when indifference is present, it doesn't necessarily mean that the Yellow will end the relationship immediately. Sometimes they'll stay because of their strong sense of responsibility or because they believe that their partner can't survive without them. If a Yellow does choose to remain when the feelings of love are gone, they'll usually bury themselves in work and find reasons to not go home rather than creating an emotionally confrontational situation.

Yellow's Expression of Love's Many Splendors

Romance

Romance for a Yellow is a mind game, so it requires their mind to be clear of distractions and focused on their relationship. They enjoy contemplating how they'd romance their partner and what they'd do to create the perfect romantic interlude. Harnessing their imagination, they create imaginary conversations, fabricate ways to exchange physical pleasures, and then mentally play out the scenarios over and over again.

This mental romantic foreplay is a good news/bad news situation for their partner. The bright side is that when the Yellow does decide to outwardly express what they've created in their mind, it will be well thought out and well orchestrated, with every detail taken into consideration. But unfortunately, they live and enjoy it so much in their mind that they don't always follow through in real life, which can leave their partner wondering if they have a romantic bone in their body.

When Yellows do decide to express themselves romantically, it may not be what their partner perceives as being romantic, because these personalities like to do things that aren't typical. Yellows see being romantic as doing thoughtful things. However, thoughtful doesn't necessarily mean showing emotions, but might mean letting their partner know that they're thinking about them.

Another loving gesture to a Yellow is buying something that they think their partner would like, could use, or would enjoy. Gifts might be a computer program, kitchen gadget, high-tech toy, new garden cart, or car-cleaning kit—all of which are intended to help solve problems and increase productivity. They're not inclined to get items that they view as nonfunctional or clutter. When they do purchase keepsakes or anything with emotional value, they intend for the gift to express how they feel without them having to say the words.

If Yellows do choose to reach out romantically, but for whatever reason don't get the feedback they desire or expect, they'll take it as a personal rejection and will not only mentally and emotionally shut down their desire for romance, they'll also forgo future displays of such sentiments. It's helpful to remember that Yellows need to be appreciated, too, and want to be praised for their sensitivity. Just because they may not express themselves emotionally doesn't mean that they can't be easily hurt.

Passion

Passion and anticipation are the same in the Yellow's mind. They see this splendor as preparation for the anticipated exchange of sexual pleasures. This color loves sensual kisses, their mate flirting with them and verbally tantalizing their mind with visual possibilities, the intertwining of bodies, caressing and stroking their partner, and snuggling. Passionate gestures feed the fantasies of the Yellow's mind and give them something to think about long after the heat of the moment has worn off.

They can't conceive of being in a relationship lacking this splendor. They need it to help them mentally shift gears before sexual intercourse and to sustain their desire for intimacy. They see passion as the emotional bond between two people and use it to reinforce their commitment to the relationship and rekindle their love for their partner. For the Yellow, romantic impulses, sexual nuances, and passionate gestures are more for the benefit of their mind than for meeting the needs of their body.

Intimacy

Out of the four expressions of intimacy—physical, emotional, mental, and spiritual—Yellows ranked mental the highest and emotional the lowest. When I asked them to describe their perception of what the former meant, they described it as being mentally in sync with their partner, understanding how the other person thinks, being familiar with the positions they'd take on things, knowing how they'd react in any given situation, and being able to read their partner's thoughts and finish their sentences. They described this quality as an unspoken bond, bringing the elements of completeness, connectivity, equanimity, and trustworthiness—all of which are important to this color.

Yellows see mental intimacy as creating a sacred space where dreams can be shared and philosophical conversations can take place without fear of criticism or rejection. As a matter of fact, some of their most mentally intimate moments are when they're sharing their thoughts while intertwined in the arms of those they love. They value the stillness and quietness of mental intimacy, and love that it's okay to be contemplative and not have to verbalize everything they're feeling inside.

Sex

Sex begins between the Yellow's ears long before it gets between the sheets. They enjoy fantasizing, anticipating, and conjuring up possibilities of what they'll experience physically. By fully engaging their mind in the sexual process, they're able to intensify their physical sensations, thus enhancing their enjoyment. Yellows are very skillful and competent lovers. They pride themselves on the creative and ingenious ways that they're able to give their partner pleasure. They're sensitive and considerate and won't do anything that will make the other person uncomfortable or leave them feeling emotionally or physically compromised. They'll go slowly until they get the indicators that their partner is enjoying themselves.

While Yellows are personally open to trying new positions or sex aids, they won't insist on either one unless their partner verbally expresses their desire to try something new. This color has a heightened sensitivity because their primary motivation in bed is to give pleasure. Consequently, they're not going to push themselves on their partner or let their own biological needs dictate anything. Yellows believe that sexuality and the sharing of pleasures should be a mutual desire, one where they can both enjoy the experience. They see this splendor as an element of what sustains a healthy, loving relationship, and think that it exemplifies the true expression of love.

Abstinence is emotionally destructive to a Yellow and can undermine their self-esteem, make them surly and contentious, or drive them to seek sexual pleasures elsewhere. It can ultimately make them end a relationship, even though they may still have strong feelings for their partner. The reason that abstinence drives them away isn't the obvious one—that is, that their sexual needs aren't being met. Instead, it's because abstinence implies sexual dissatisfaction, which in turn implies rejection. This means personal failure and signifies that they've not only let their partner down, they've failed themselves as well. Yellows are their own greatest enemy through the high expectations they put on everything they do.

Communication

Yellows perceive themselves as being good communicators and are surprised when other people don't share their same perspective. From the Yellows' point of view, they're articulate, clear, and concise in conveying their thoughts, and careful to think things through before they say them. The issue is that they spend so much time carrying on so many internal dialogues that they think they've said something when, in fact, they haven't. When this happens—which it does regularly—the Yellow becomes critical and judgmental of the other person, accusing them of not listening or not paying attention. Talk about a communication problem! It's a no-win situation for everyone, and it's a challenge for both parties to keep their cool and not become emotionally reactive. In the short term, this problem creates instant tension in the relationship, and over time, it could potentially break down the lines of communication altogether.

Yellows don't like to engage in small talk and will avoid conversations that are superficial or emotional. Instead, they prefer to involve themselves in discussions that are mentally stimulating and create the opportunity for them to share their opinions and knowledge. They enjoy identifying problems, offering solutions, and discussing concepts and ideas intended to provoke thinking. Yellows like a good debate and are known to belabor a point if they think that someone isn't getting what they're trying to say. They can manipulate conversations masterfully to achieve their ends and will become verbose and nitpicky when they think they're right and you're wrong, although their breadth of knowledge and use of words make them engaging conversationalists.

Commitment

Yellows generally suffer from commitment anxiety, meaning that they have a tendency to avoid committing until they're sure that they can completely trust someone with their heart. Entering into a relationship means taking on the responsibility for another person's emotional well-being, which they perceive as a high price to pay. They understand very well that they have trouble with their own needs without taking on someone else's, too. The word *commitment* stereotypically represents the loss of personal freedom, and Yellows aren't interested in doing this. Traditionally, personal identity is sacrificed for the purpose of creating a new identity as a couple. Again, this isn't their idea of a good time. This applies to both males and females.

The ideal commitment scenario for the Yellow is one where they feel accepted for who they are and their nonconformist nature is perceived as a strength. They want a partner who's not interested in changing them or converting them over to their way of thinking. Yellows are looking for someone who will dedicate themselves to making things work but won't lose their identity in the process. They want all of the benefits of love without the complicated expectations associated with commitment. While Yellows believe in the sanctity of matrimony, they don't believe that it ensures that a union will endure over the course of time. That's why it's not uncommon to find Yellows in the same relationship for many years and yet still not married.

Commitment must be the Yellow's idea, because they want to be sure that they're truly ready. Unlike the other personality colors, Yellows can't and won't be pushed, coerced, intimidated, emotionally manipulated, or even seduced into making a commitment until it becomes acceptable to them. Even ultimatums won't work, and in fact will have the opposite effect, causing them to pull away.

When I asked the Yellows what determines when they're ready, they said that it's when they feel they can completely trust a person with their heart and believe that they've found the person they want to spend the rest of their life with. Yellows see making a commitment as giving their word to love and honor their partner forever—never as a casual interlude. Consequently, any commitment they do make is as solid as the Rock of Gibraltar.

How Love Changes with Age

Love takes on new meaning as Yellows age. It becomes more important to them as they begin to realize how it adds to the quality of their lives and fulfills their inner emotional needs. Their desire to be alone becomes less tolerable, and their need to have a permanent someone in their life increases. If a Yellow is in a relationship, they experience a newfound appreciation for their partner and what they bring to the union. If they aren't with anyone, the thought of being alone in their old age is less appealing, and they find themselves experiencing moments of loneliness and melancholy. Yellows enjoy traveling and experiencing new things, so as they age their need for a companion with whom to share those things overrides their commitment anxiety.

In their 40s, Yellows become less intense and singularly focused on their professional life. They find that the goals they set in their 20s and 30s become less important as their need to find balance drives much of what they do. They find themselves wanting to spend more time with their partner just playing and enjoying each other's company.

Yellow start asking themselves, *What really matters?* and *Is this all there is?* Even though they're deep thinkers, younger Yellows don't spend much time being contemplative, yet when they hit their midlife crises somewhere in their mid-40s, suddenly being introspective has a different appeal. They start to realize how important their relationships are to them, and look for ways to make up for lost time. At this age, Yellows start questioning why they've been so afraid to enter into emotional commitments. They find themselves caught on the horns of a dilemma as they discover that they really don't understand themselves emotionally at all, and have no idea how to get in touch with their inner feelings.

Their 50s are a pivotal time for Yellows as they realize how seriously they've taken life, and how their sense of responsibility has driven them to stay in jobs they didn't like or kept them in relationships that were unfulfilling. They become restless and seek friendships and activities to fill the void and put excitement back into their lives. And while work is still their primary focus, it becomes less important as they understand that work can't satisfy their emotional needs or keep them warm at night.

If a Yellow is in a relationship at this age, they'll seek ways to develop emotional intimacy and will become more emotionally expressive. They'll be less judgmental and more tolerant of other people's faults. Their aloofness will diminish and they'll become more approachable. And, instead of avoiding emotional conversations, they'll actually welcome the opportunity to share their feelings.

While Yellows do mellow to some extent as they age, the expectations they have of themselves don't. Even in their 60s and 70s, their need to prove that they're not getting old drives them. Yellows will push themselves to do the same things they did in earlier years, only now they'll want to do them better. They believe that age is merely a state of mind, and their mind isn't going to let them age gracefully. The Yellow's perspective on growing old is that they'll never retire or stop pushing themselves to fulfill their potential.

Yellow's Fears, Insecurities, and Anxieties

Yellows are natural leaders and pride themselves on their ability to handle whatever life throws them with ease, confidence, and grace. The Orange and Green personalities see the Yellow as being strong and capable of protecting them from the unpleasantness of life. Yet under their outer persona of confidence are fears, insecurities, and anxieties, which cause them to feel emotionally vulnerable. The only difference between the Yellow and the other personality colors is that they won't let anyone get close enough to discover those vulnerabilities. Here are some of the emotional issues a Yellow keeps hidden inside:

- Fear of being responsible for other people's emotional well-being

- Fear of being accountable for what they can't control

- Fear of failure

- Fear of being trapped in an emotionally needy and volatile relationship

- Resentment of relationships that aren't equitable and where they must carry the burden of responsibility for those who aren't willing to take care of themselves

- Fear of having their emotional vulnerabilities used against them

- General lack of trust

- Fear of being seen as stupid or incompetent

- Inability to express feelings

- Fear of making a wrong decision

- Fear of being criticized or caught unprepared

- Frustration about being responsible for other people's mistakes

- Inability to shed tears or express remorse

The Evolutionary Stage of a Relationship That Yellows Are Most Attracted To

The stage most appealing to the Yellow personality is growing together as a couple. And even though it may take time before they actually make a commitment, once they do, they look forward to spending their life with a partner who grows into their best friend. Yellows enjoy the stability of a long-term relationship and get pleasure from the intimacy that comes from years of learning more about the other person. There's a sense of comfort for the Yellow in knowing that they're with someone who will be there for them, and who knows them so intimately that they can anticipate their needs. In the Yellow's mind, they can see themselves laughing, loving, and still sexually pursuing their partner late into their golden years.

The Evolutionary Stage of a Relationship That's Most Difficult for a Yellow

We certainly covered this topic thoroughly when we looked at the Yellows' commitment anxiety! However, there's another stage that's difficult for the Yellow, and that's dating. Their intolerance for small talk makes this stage a problem, as does their knee-jerk need to help other people solve problems by telling them what they should do. While appearing confident on the outside, a Yellow's fear of rejection causes them to avoid situations where they don't feel secure and confident, and dating certainly puts them in that environment.

Putting together a relationship is awkward for them, as it brings their emotional inadequacies and insecurities to the surface, leaving them unsure of how they should act or what they should say. If at all possible, Yellows will avoid a blind date because they're generally uneasy with strangers and realize that their aloofness makes them hard to get to know. They'd much rather date someone they've already met and are familiar with, such as a co-worker, a friend, or someone from church. At least in this kind of setup, there's some kind of history with the other person, and they already know what their date is interested in.

Overview of the Yellow Personality	
Basic needs:	• Independence and autonomy
	• Sought out for their competency and expertise
	• Relationships void of emotional complexity or neediness
	• The opportunity to share their problem-solving skills, knowledge, and opinions
Emotional needs:	• Mutual respect and commitment
	• Shared values and principles
	• Intellectual stimulation
	• Truthfulness, emotional sensitivity, and trust
Key strengths:	• Leadership skills and take-charge attitude
	• High standards and integrity
	• Visionary skills and the ability to anticipate future problems
	• Strong sense of responsibility and the need to protect those they love
Key weaknesses:	• Inability to express themselves emotionally
	• Spending too much time thinking and preparing rather than taking action
	• Suspicious, skeptical, and untrusting
	• Brooding and self-destructive when expectations aren't met

Overview of the Yellow Personality, cont'd.	
Primary fear:	• Being accountable for someone else's shortcomings
Attracted to people who are:	• Self-confident and self-reliant
	• Intelligent and mentally stimulating
	• Fellow Yellows
Dislike people who are:	• Emotionally insensitive, needy, and unwilling to take control of their lives
	• High maintenance, and who don't keep their word
	• Unpredictable, unorganized, and focused solely on themselves
	• Always late
Relationship expectations:	• Truthfulness, trustworthiness, and faithfulness
	• Sensitivity to their need for quiet, alone time
	• Sharing of responsibilities
Value in a relationship:	• Friendship, companionship, and partnership
Room for improvement:	• Takes life too seriously and sees only the problems
	• Communicating what they're thinking
	• Expressing what they're feeling
Annoyances:	• Being pressed to make a decision before they have time to think it through thoroughly
Causes of stress:	• Trying to control the unknown
Relationship challenge:	• Making an emotional commitment
	• Trusting someone with their heart

Hot Tips for Dealing with Yellows	
Love	Tell them how proud you are of them and how much you admire their thinking. Voice your respect and appreciation.
Romance	Do thoughtful things that send the message you're thinking about them. Tell them how much you love them.
Passion	Entice them mentally with suggestive temptations such as a good, long, sensual kiss.
Sex	Seduce their minds by sharing what you'd like to do to them sexually.
Communication	Keep discussions thought provoking and interesting. Avoid emotionally charged conversations.

Helpful Hints for Yellows in Dealing with Other Personality Colors	
Love	Don't let your overly protective nature become smothering. Remember to say "I love you."
Romance	Reach out emotionally and give your partner what they need romantically, such a hug, a kiss, one-on-one time, or your undivided attention.
Passion	Tell your partner how much you desire them and how much they turn you on.
Sex	Don't assume that your partner is always in the mood for sex. Ask if and when they'll be interested.
Communication	Avoid letting your mind wander in a conversation and be sensitive to the fact that questioning can be seen as either needing more information or challenging someone's decision.

CHAPTER EIGHT

The Green Personality:
The "Let's-Experience-It-All" People

*C*arey has worked as a postal clerk for years and has been in the same position, at the same branch location, and even in the same small space in the back of the building for longer than she'd like to admit. When I asked her how, as an extroverted Green personality, she has put up with it for so long and dealt with the isolation, I truthfully expected a flood of emotions to spew forth. I thought that she'd tell me how lonely she was, how frustrating it was to be in such a redundant job pattern, and how unhappy she was wasting her life away doing something for money that she didn't love.

What I heard was something totally different. She acknowledged that the job was boring and said she did miss being with people. However, she went on to say that it was really a gift in disguise because it let her do what she really loved the most: dancing. When I asked her to explain, she told me that she lived in a very small apartment, so there wasn't any room for her to move around and practice her dance steps. And besides, her neighbors complained about all of the thumping and jumping. At work, because of where she was located in the back of the post office, there was plenty of room for her to dance.

Carey described how she'd choreograph her routines while sorting mail and then rehearse them as she put the letters in the correct *distribution areas. Because there wasn't anyone to distract, she could move around freely. I asked how her boss liked her dancing at work, and the fact that she wore a headset to listen to her music. She said that it was fine, as long as she did her job.*

So there she was, dancing her way through the day—doing what she loved and getting paid at the same time. What more is there? I could see what she meant by the job being a gift. At the same time, I couldn't help but think how only a Green could turn what would appear to the other personality colors to be an unexciting, boring, dead-end job into something that was fun and gave her what she needed to accomplish her life's dream.

A General Description of the Green Personality

Greens are dreamers and have rich, vivid imaginations. They're the free spirits of the personality world who march to their own drummers and are naturally hopeful and optimistic. They focus on the positive aspects of life, and tend to see only the good in people. When something negative does happen to a Green, they'll immediately try to find the lesson in it. Once they do so, they'll use it as a catalyst for change, transforming their behavior, appearance, friends, job, and even their relationships.

Greens love change and actually seek it. They don't think it's negative, but rather see it as being a necessary component of personal growth and the motivator to fix what isn't working in their life. While this works for their personality, it can be very disruptive to other people, especially their mate, because it creates a certain amount of turmoil and chaos and keeps the relationship in a constant state of flux.

When I asked some mates of Greens about this color's need for variety, they unanimously agreed that the change itself isn't a problem. The issue is that Greens don't know how to moderate the process, meaning that they don't transform just one thing at a time and wait for the dust to settle; they switch everything all at once. Some of their mates even said that their greatest concern about living with their Green was wondering if they or their relationship was in jeopardy every time things got tossed around. Because of this color's propensity for sudden bursts of change, other personalities tend to see them as loose cannons; and as being flighty, fickle, and indecisive.

Greens are the cheerleaders of the personality world, and their optimistic "can-do" attitude makes them natural motivators. "Live your dream" is their mantra, and they'll use it to inspire and encourage others to do the same. Yet while Greens are quick to help other people discover their hidden strengths and talents, they tend to have difficulty finding their own. They struggle with the challenges of life and are always looking for ways to improve themselves. They're perennial students and are drawn to books, workshops, and classes that will help them better cope with life, teach them how to create more loving relationships, offer ways to be more effective at expressing themselves, and encourage the development of their spiritual nature.

The Green's days must have meaning and purpose. They seek to understand the intricacies of life and discover their life's work, and their quest to learn more about themselves will often take them off the beaten path. Consequently, it isn't unusual for them to become involved in esoteric studies; practice the beliefs of other cultures; or explore mysticism, the occult, and metaphysics. The New Age movement provides a safe haven for Greens to find themselves, express their uniqueness, and experiment with their nontraditional ways of experiencing life. At the same time, it puts them with people who are like-minded, sharing similar values and their quest to discover who they really are. Life is a mystery to Greens, and they're intrigued with the idea that they chose this time in the evolution of consciousness to be a part of the world.

Greens possess the gift of highly developed intuition and are able to sense the "vibes" of what's going on around them. This extrasensory aspect of their personality allows them to read between the lines and know how people are feeling. It helps them gain clarity in a situation so that they can uncover hidden agendas and distance themselves from the potential for conflict. Their intuitiveness changes their perception of reality and makes it possible for them to see their connection with all that exists. These qualities make them interesting conversationalists and fun people to be around.

There are two speeds at which Greens live their lives: full speed ahead or completely shut down. When they're in the first mode, it isn't unusual for them to have multiple sentences going at one time and not to finish one before moving on to the next. It's also likely that they won't finish what they've started, as they're trying to spin many plates all at one time. On the other hand, when they're shut down, you could scrape them off the floor with a putty knife, and there's no motivating them to do anything. They're so energetically out of gas that they just want to be left alone. Even the introverted Greens, whose tendency is to conserve their energy, find themselves falling victim to their desire to do it all, have it all, and experience it all.

Creative is the word that best describes Greens. They tend to be artists, poets, writers, actors, and musicians. They're constantly looking for new and different ways to express their individuality, whether it's through their work, play, hobbies, or relationships. Greens have many talents, and their greatest challenge is learning to focus on one at a time.

Seeing things to completion isn't one of the Greens' strengths. The cliché "jack-of-all-trades and master of none" certainly fits them because of their tendency to not stay with anything long enough to truly perfect it. Their creative restlessness also leads them to believe that the grass is always greener on the other side of the fence. As a result, they constantly want to be on that "other side."

Boredom is a continual problem for this color, so they'll try hard to avoid redundancy, whether it's doing the same thing, having sex the same way, or staying with someone too long. Once the relationship becomes boring, they may seek to find adventure and excitement with someone else.

Greens are emotional people who wear their hearts on their sleeves. They'll give 110 percent of themselves if they believe that it will give them the love they need. They don't have any problem sharing how or what they're feeling, and tend to get their feelings hurt easily.

Greens also don't like conflict. Unlike Oranges, however, they won't stuff their emotions for very long before they have to get them off their chest. When they do, they're neither timid nor meek, and they won't leave you wondering whether you hit their hot button. How can you tell you've pushed a Green too far? First, their voice will go up several octaves, and then lovely four-letter words will roll off their tongue—and I don't mean the word *love*. When their feelings are hurt or they're angry, these fun-loving, easygoing personalities will become aggressive and have no qualms about using salty language.

Greens are the chameleons of the personality world, meaning that they have the ability to be so flexible and adaptable that they look and act like different personality colors. And while this quality makes them likable, it also has its downside. The first problem is that they can be difficult to live with, because their mate never knows how they'll act or where they're coming from. When they're in their Green mode, they're fun, playful, and easy to get along with. When they go Red, they're argumentative, aggressive, and contentious. When they're Orange, they're moody, suffer from martyrdom, and become self-righteous. And when they turn Yellow, they're stubborn, challenging, defiant, and nonconforming.

Ten Observable Behavioral Traits of a Green Personality

Here are ten of the most observable behavioral traits of the Green personality. Each one contributes to the Greens' creativity and fun-loving nature. Although other personality colors may display what appears to be similar behavior, a Green will demonstrate these behaviors more consistently and frequently.

1. Expressive. Greens are emotionally expressive and aren't shy about public displays of affection. They love to verbally state how much they love someone and to show how much they care. Because Greens make decisions emotionally, it's important for them to convey *what* they're feeling, *how* they're feeling, and *why* they're feeling that way. This also lets them observe other people's emotional reactions and use them to determine how to act.

2. Idealistic. Greens live in a world of hopes and dreams, and have an idealistic perspective of what life should be. They believe that in a perfect world everyone should get along with each other and love should be unconditional. They're so driven by their idealism that it's a constant struggle for them to not lose touch with reality—a common feeling that Greens express when they say they need to be more grounded.

3. Attention seeking. Greens love to be the center of attention and will use their dramatic flair for style to help them stand out in a crowd. Oblivious to conventionality, they create interesting and eccentric behavior to get other people to notice them. They're very conscientious about their grooming and appearance, and have been known to dress in wild and outrageous clothing just to see the shocked looks on other people's faces.

4. Cheerleading. The Greens' enthusiasm for life coupled with their ability to turn the ordinary into the extraordinary make them enjoyable to be around. They're the pied pipers of the personality world. The primary motivation behind the things they do is encouraging people to feel good about themselves, cheering people on when they're feeling down, and sharing the message of love. Greens arouse excitement and energize and charm people into wanting to let go of their fears, drop their guard, and open their hearts up to whatever experiences life offers.

5. Active. Both introverted and extroverted Greens seem to have boundless amounts of energy. They're active, busy people who prefer to keep moving rather than staying stuck in one place. "A rolling stone gathers no moss" best describes the Green's insatiable need to participate in whatever sounds fun. They believe that life should be enjoyed. To them, that means days rich with activities involving loved ones, having fun, and communing with nature.

6. Intuitive. Because Greens rely primarily on the right hemisphere of their brain for gathering information (intuition) and making decisions (emotions), they're masterful at creating a holistic picture of what's really going on. Greens tend to trust their hunches and goose bumps rather than relying on logic or following what's obvious. Their uncanny ability to read people and know intuitively how they're feeling makes it difficult to hide anything from them.

7. Creative. Greens love to brainstorm, create ideas, and play out possibilities. They're imaginative, witty, unconventional, enterprising, and continually coming up with new ways to do things. They're bold and adventurous and thrive in environments where their abilities are appreciated. Since Greens see the world through the right half of the brain, they're not bound by the limitations or mental barriers associated with the left side (which is primarily logical and analytical). Consequently, they're able to allow their creativity to flow freely and to come up with groundbreaking ideas.

8. Unpredictable. Greens are emotionally unpredictable and moody. When they're in love and happy in their relationships, they're fun to be around. Their enthusiasm for life is contagious, and their flair is inspiring. They're optimistic, playful, and willing to go with the flow. When they're in an emotional funk, however, they're moody, difficult to be around, cold, distant, and argumentative. They'll tend to read negative meanings into everything that's said and done, and will be contrary and stubborn. Because of this, other people see them as fickle and difficult to live with, and will want to avoid them until they come back to their normal cheerful selves.

9. Changeable. Just when it looks like a Green is finally settling down and focusing their attention on one thing, they'll throw a curveball by suddenly deciding to do something different. While their tendency is to modify what isn't working, it's not unlike them to shake up what *is* going well when they get bored. This allows Greens to use their creativity and experience new things. Since they struggle with boredom, they'll use change as a means of adding spice to their life.

10. Adaptable. Greens are spontaneous, flexible, and open to trying new things. They're attracted to experiences that allow them to be different from the norm and that support the abstract way they see the world. Greens thrive in relationships where they have the freedom to be themselves and to march to their own drummer. They're easygoing and are usually able to fit into any situation comfortably. It's simple for them to adjust to whatever is demanded of them, and their cooperative nature makes them good team players. They harness their adaptability in the creative things they do, and see it as one of their greatest assets.

What Love Means to a Green

Love is like a celestial event for the Green—a sacred cosmic union and a harmonic convergence of the mind and body. It represents the merging of hearts, spirits, and souls and seems to magically transform two people into one. Greens experience love deeply and simultaneously, meaning physically, emotionally, mentally, and spiritually all at the same time. They see this as an opportunity to form a significant spiritual connection with someone they care for deeply. They believe that love creates the fertile environment where two people can grow personally and spiritually and revel in all its inherent splendors. Greens romanticize, idealize, and fantasize about love, thus creating illusions about how it should be. They use their vivid imaginations to play out how they'll feel and act when in love, and what life will be like when they find their soul mate.

Greens have high expectations and demand much from the people who love them. Many of their expectations tend to be unrealistic and as a result leave them unsatisfied and emotionally unfulfilled. Greens believe that love should shelter them from the unpleasantness of life and protect them from other people's insensitivities and hostility. They think it will somehow transform them into the person they want to be, rather than who they really are. They want it to rescue them from their feelings of despair and their fear of being alone, to transmute the mundane aspects of life, and to magically transform their lives into a Cinderella story. They depend on this emotion to fulfill their deepest inner emotional needs and to feed them spiritually.

Greens have a difficult time accepting that love can't meet all their expectations, and rather than looking inward to find out why, they'll blame their mate for not giving them what they want. They aren't willing to address the issue that perhaps their unrealistic expectations and illusions are setting them up for heartache and causing them to never find the love they long for.

The Greens' need to be the center of attention and share their feelings can be very demanding on a relationship and their mate. They insist that their partner view them as the most important person in their life and expect them to be completely devoted and to dote on them. They want their mate to make them feel special and indulge them with gifts and time. They feel most loved when their lover is attentive to their needs, showers them with compliments, and puts them on a pedestal. This color wants to be admired for their creativity, embraced for their emotional sensitivity, and to have their emotional needs put above all else.

Greens can be possessive and jealous, and will become resentful of people and situations that exclude them from sharing time or activities with their mate. They get their feelings hurt easily if their mate suggests doing things separately. In their need to feel loved, the Green craves total togetherness, doing and sharing everything as one. They want to know all about their partner, including what they're thinking; how they're feeling; their dreams, fears, vulnerabilities, and insecurities; and their innermost secrets. The problem is that when their mate *does* share all of those things in the name of love, the Green will use this knowledge against him or her when the conversations become hurtful, and then try to "guilt" the other person back into loving them.

Greens love deeply, boldly, aggressively, and flamboyantly; and can take the act of being in love and turn it into a grand, spectacular, and mystical experience. They want all of their love stories to have happy endings and long to live happily ever after. They believe that love is what life's all about, and see it as their purpose to give, create, express, and teach love—and show others how to find it. This might help explain why their interactions with people always seem to be focused on creating meaningful and lasting relationships.

Greens have the ability to make love fun and to make life exciting. They're all heart and are masterful at transforming affection into a higher art form. They see it as their mission in life to continually come up with creative ways to express their emotions and show just how much they care. This can make them very appealing, which is why the Red personality is attracted to them like a moth to a flame.

Green's Expression of Love's Many Splendors

Romance

Greens are truly both the *hopeless* and *hopeful* romantics of the personality world. The former label indicates the fact that they're sentimental, openly romantic, demonstrative, and easily moved by any gestures that say "I love you." A rose on their pillow, a sentimental song, or a mushy card can win over their heart.

They're also *hopeful,* because they're eternally optimistic that they'll find their magical mate. They hope that once they discover that special person, their life will be transformed into the perfect love story. Greens adore romance in every sense of the word, and out of love's many splendors, they excel the most in this one. They see this quality as creating the opportunity for a deeper sense of intimacy and solidifying their emotional connection with their mate.

For Greens, the word *romance* conjures up images of the celestial merging of souls, an arrow from Cupid's bow, sailing off into the sunset, and Scarlett O'Hara running into the arms of her beloved Rhett. This splendor stimulates their imagination and turns on their creativity, thus inspiring them to concoct scenarios that are outrageous, outlandish, adventurous, and even bizarre. Greens see romance as being limitless and place no boundaries on themselves. It's not unlike them to whisk that special someone off to a secluded hideaway to spend hours—or even days—just enjoying the pleasure of each other's company.

Greens enjoy strolls on the beach, midnight rendezvous, candlelit dinners, cuddling in front of a fireplace, watching romantic movies, conversations over morning coffee, dancing, art shows, antique fairs, shopping, flying kites, skydiving, nature adventures, traveling, and experiencing new things. The most desirable romantic activities for this color are those that encourage closeness and focus primarily on just being together. The way the Green sees it is that as long as they're with the person they care about, doing what they love, life is good, and abundant happiness will be enjoyed by all.

Greens excel at using romantic gestures to seduce, entice, excite, and prevent their relationships from falling into the humdrum patterns. Keep in mind that they love anything outlandish, outrageous, and flamboyant. It isn't beyond them to create scenarios intended to surprise and even shock their mate just to ensure that they know how much they're desired. Greens will do things such as presenting themselves wrapped in a bow for their mate's birthday, showing up in a long coat with nothing on underneath, or dressing up as an exotic dancer in order to get their partner's attention. Greens are huggers, hand holders, arm wrappers, body drapers, and kissing machines who enjoy any display of affection.

Passion

On the list of what's important to Greens in their relationship, passion ranks very high. They see it as an essential element in the development of emotional intimacy, and believe that when there isn't an open expression of passion, it's difficult—if not impossible—to create the connection needed to sustain a lasting relationship. They believe this quality is responsible for keeping the flames of love burning brightly in their heart, and enjoy anything associated with being passionate, such as sensual kissing, the whispering of sweet words, caressing each other's bodies, and indulging all of the five senses. They delight in erotic activities and uncon-ventional expressions that give pleasure to the physical body and feed their fantasies. They perceive passion as doing things that are provocative, playful, and conducive to sharing sexual pleasure. They'll use this splendor as a way of communicating their desire and devotion, and ensuring that their mate will remain faithful.

Intimacy

Greens see intimacy as the true essence of love and the glue that holds the relationship together. It's a way to get in touch with their deep inner emotional needs. This splendor allows them to love freely, giving them the closeness they need in order to feel secure in their relationship and to heal old emotional wounds. As a transformational tool, Greens use intimacy as a means of letting go of the fears they have about being alone and not being worthy of affection. They use it to open up their heart to trusting love and other people, and they see it as forming the emotional and spiri-tual connection they need in order to remain committed.

The Green's need for intimacy overshadows all of the other splendors of love because they believe that without the bond it creates, none of the other splendors can be honestly expressed. When asked to rank the four expressions of intimacy (physical, emotional, mental, and spiritual), the Greens consistently ranked spiritual intimacy first and emotional intimacy second, and the physical aspect was third. Mental closeness was at the bottom of the list, which most Greens said was because they really weren't interested in being mentally in sync with their mate or knowing what they thought; this color would rather know what someone is feeling.

Greens love the concept of spiritual intimacy because it repre-sents entwined hearts and the merging of souls. It's necessary for the creation of a new identity and reflects the process of becoming one with their mate. They adore thinking that they were spiritu-ally predestined to be with their mate, and that their love was mystically created in the heavens. They see spiritual closeness as a sacred, unspoken truth and a way to share life with someone who shares their esoteric beliefs and philosophies. It confirms their connection to all that exists and places value on being a steward of the earth, saving the animals, and honoring the needs of the less fortunate. They believe that spiritual intimacy supports unconditional love and creates a safe place where feelings, thoughts, and unorthodox perceptions can be shared without fear of retaliation—where it's okay to discuss the things near and dear to their heart, such as metaphysical studies, energy, holistic medicine, and the connection between themselves, God, heaven, and angels.

Sex

Sex for the Green isn't just physical; it's also an emotional experience. They see it as the consecration of their commitment and an expression of how much they value their relationship. Sex is an integral part of their communication process because it conveys their emotional needs without them having to say the words. Sex allows them to share their feelings, express their pleasure by making guttural sounds and moaning with ecstasy, and use their body to tell their mate how much they're enjoying the physical sensations they're experiencing. This splendor is a cosmic intertwining of their hearts and souls. It's a way to connect with their mate on a deeper level and physically express the needs of their spirit. Sex energizes and revitalizes this color, banishing the emptiness that they experience when separated from the one they love.

For Greens, sex is more than just intercourse. It's the enjoyment of all aspects of the physical: looking deeply into their lover's eyes, sounds of pleasure, the scent of each other, caresses, and sensations of arousal that come from long kisses. Greens enjoy foreplay and need it to help get them in the mood. For them, it includes sharing what turns them on and hearing about what excites their mate. They don't like this part of sex to be rushed, but instead want it drawn out until they almost reach the point of climax—then they're ready to make love.

Once sex is over, the Greens like to be complimented on their skills and have their mate share how much they enjoyed the experience. Greens want to bask in the afterglow as long as possible, and post-sex conversations help them accomplish this. That's why they aren't quick to jump up, but would rather lie there and talk. If this color could create the perfect lovemaking interlude, they'd spend all day lying in their mate's arms and avoiding the demands of life altogether.

Communication

Greens believe that the quality of their relationship is directly connected to the caliber of their communication. In other words, this splendor can either make or break their relationship. When the lines are open, everything flows smoothly and they feel good about it. But when communication breaks down, so do the feelings they have for their mate and their desire to be with them. However, the process can be tricky with a Green, as it's difficult to read where they are emotionally. They're very good at giving off the illusion that everything is fine when actually it isn't. To be an effective communicator with this color, you have to develop the ability to read nonverbal signs, such as body language and eye contact, and not just rely on what you hear. You have to watch for the telltale warning signs alerting you that there's unhappiness brewing inside.

While Greens are unpredictable in many things, they're extremely predictable when it comes to the communication process. First, when they're happy and feel good about themselves and their relationship, the conversations are upbeat, positive, and focused on the future. They're entertaining and encourage both talking and listening. Second, they'll always speak from their heart and expect their mate to do the same. If they don't feel that their mate has done this, they become distressed, disappointed, angry, and might even feel betrayed.

If they're unhappy, the conversations will mostly consist of listening to them get their feelings off their chest. If they're feeling mistreated or underappreciated, they'll become cold, silent, and avoid any conversation or interaction at all. The best thing to do when this happens is to address the problem immediately. Don't try to ignore it, dismiss it, or sweep it under the rug in the hopes that it will go away. Don't just chalk it up to their having another emotional meltdown. And most important, even if you might be thinking it, *never ever* utter the words "There you go being emotional again." A comment like this could land you in the doghouse for hours or days—even weeks.

Greens are very effective at using the silent treatment to get the point across that you've said or done something that hurt their feelings. The best way to handle a communication crisis such as this is to encourage them to share how they're feeling and ask them to tell you what you did wrong so that you can avoid repeating it in the future. This approach will immediately defuse the situation and once again open up the lines of communication.

Here are a few other mistakes when communicating with a Green:

- Treating them impersonally
- Using a condescending tone of voice
- Making patronizing comments
- Talking about them as if they aren't there

All of these situations will upset them and set off a barrage of unpleasant reactions, which can range from merely expressing their displeasure to shouting, or being verbally cruel. It's best to remember that when it comes to communicating Greens are binary, meaning that they're either responsive or reactive.

Commitment

When Greens were asked about commitment, their responses fell into two distinct categories:

1. They don't need a commitment because then it's easier to walk away from a relationship that's not working.

2. A commitment is absolutely necessary if they're going to feel secure in a relationship and have it endure over the years.

When I asked for more clarification from the Greens who gave the first answer, many said that having a commitment didn't ensure that the relationship would last, and besides, it complicates things. Some explained that they would stay in a relationship, committed or not, as long as it met their expectations, was fun, and fulfilled their emotional and sexual needs. Others wanted the freedom to enjoy the opposite sex outside of their own relationship, and felt that a commitment took away this freedom. Yet another group believed that the price they'd have to pay because of a commitment would be too high.

All of them agreed that the word *commitment* felt stifling and restrictive and was more of a detriment to a relationship than a benefit. What this group's response supports is that Greens don't see having frequent, short-term relationships as negative, and they prefer to keep their options open just in case someone more suited to them comes along—someone who might be their soul mate, and who's spiritually in sync with them.

Then there were the Greens who gave the second answer. They explained that a commitment provided the security they needed from a relationship and ensured that their physical and emotional needs would be met. Some believed that love can only be *true* love when there's a commitment from both people to making it work. Still others said that without the bond created by a commitment, the door was open to infidelity and extramarital affairs. All of this group agreed that a one-sided commitment, or the lack of any official obligation, spelled trouble.

The primary issue Greens have around the word *commitment* is that the element of control comes with it, leaving them vulnerable to other people trying to dictate what they can do. These personalities have a natural aversion to anyone or anything that tries to run their lives. They want the freedom to do what they want, when they want.

Over the years, I've watched an interesting phenomenon take place that supports the saying "Opposites attract." This is the fact that Reds are strongly attracted to this color. It appears that they're intrigued by the Greens because they're so passionate about life, open to new experiences, and willing to take risks. They're less rigid and more adaptable, and embrace change rather than avoiding it or allowing it to consume them with fear. Reds get tired of always having to work and carry the burden of responsibility for those they love. Deep inside, the Reds desire to be more joyful and develop their sense of play, and what better teacher than a Green?

However, a relationship with a Red comes with their compulsive need to be in control of both people and their environment. To say that this is a problem for a Green is an understatement! Not only does the Red's need to control drive the Green away, it causes them to become frustrated, resentful, aggressive, and even confrontational—none of which are the amicable qualities associated with the Green personality.

In the initial stages of developing a relationship, the Green enjoys the security, sex, and commitment the Red offers, and is willing to forego their need for freedom and suppress their feelings about being controlled. However, after the newness wears off and the relationship matures, the Green's tolerance to put up with the Red's idiosyncrasies quickly diminishes. Almost overnight, the Red's need to control and constant desire to know where the Green is and when they'll be back becomes burdensome. It can leave the Green wondering, *Why was I so quick to commit to a long-term relationship with such a control freak?*

How Love Changes with Age

The Green's illusions about what love should be, and what true love means, don't change as they age. They're still as much the proverbial romantics at age 60 as they were in their late teens. What *does* change is their tolerance to put up with other people's behavior that causes them to compromise who they are or that makes them feel bad about themselves.

Somewhere in their 30s, Greens go through a transitional stage and realize that their life isn't what they wanted it to be. At this age, they're less inclined to idealize their mate and may find themselves unhappy in their relationship or even looking outside of it to find the love they need. The initial feelings they had about their mate being the greatest person in the world settle into the realization that their partner is not only imperfect, they have a lot of burdensome emotional baggage. Unfortunately, when these revelations occur, the Green's feelings about their choice of a mate change, and not always for the better.

The 40s are an emotionally stressful time in the Green's life, as they enter the midlife-crisis zone. They begin to see how they've wasted their life doing what was necessary to survive, but didn't necessarily feed their soul. They start to recognize how much of themselves they've given up just to have a relationship and question whether it was worth it. Yet, even in this time of self-reflection, most Greens will still choose to stay in a relationship that doesn't give them the love they need. Because of all the years they've invested in it, they don't feel that they can just walk away, even though that's what they'd like to do.

Many Greens end up staying in bad or codependent relationships, and even abusive situations, because they're either afraid to leave or they believe that going will hurt their mate. Some Greens admitted that they stay in unfulfilling relationships because they truly believe that their partner can't survive without them. But no matter what the reasons, when obligation steps in and love steps out, both people lose.

At this stage in life, it also isn't uncommon to hear Greens express that they feel as if they're dying inside, and they wish that their mate could change into the person they want them to be. When Greens say that they're "dying inside," they're referring to an emotional and spiritual death, not a physical decay. However, the personality colors who take things literally—such as the Red—do believe that the Green is actually dying.

In their 50s, Greens finally settle down and start becoming more comfortable with themselves and accepting who they are. They realize that marching to their own drummer isn't such a bad thing after all, because it opens up the opportunity to grow personally and experience new things. Greens stop expecting other people to make them feel good about who they are and to comfort them emotionally. Instead, they begin to find ways to sustain themselves.

They're less inclined to work as hard at making other people happy or doing what others want. They start focusing on their own joy and doing what's important to them. At this age, Greens become more introspective and start to realize that the love they've been longing for, searching for, and needing so much isn't the affection they get from someone else—it's what they give themselves. When they discover this, they find a new appreciation for their personality and recognize how good it is to be Green.

Their early 60s find the Greens back to their old selves and looking for new opportunities, new adventures, and in some cases, even new loves. They find themselves wanting to relive their youth, to do and try everything they missed when responsibility preempted fun and self-indulgence. At this stage in life, it isn't unusual to find the Greens jumping out of airplanes, taking up new hobbies (such as dancing, painting, or playing music), or taking a trip around the world.

The zest for life they have at this age, coupled with their willingness to try new things, inspires other people to get out of their ruts and let go of whatever is holding them back from following their dreams. Greens believe that age is a state of mind, and you're only as old as you think you are. They understand that love can be found at any age—and *with* any age—so it isn't unusual to see a mature Green male or female with a younger lover. Greens pride themselves on showing other people that you're never too old to start over again . . . and never too old for sex. Their perception of life is that it begins when the kids move out, and the needs of other people no longer drive their lives or determine who they are.

Greens' Fears, Insecurities, and Anxieties

Because of their idealistic tendencies, these individuals often find themselves dismayed, overwhelmed, and distraught because the world isn't really the way they see it, and love isn't what they wanted it to be. Their heightened emotional sensitivity means that their feelings get hurt easily, and they experience much heartache throughout their lives. They fantasize about what a perfect world would be like, where people would love unconditionally and be more tolerant and accepting of each other's differences. They wonder if they'll ever find the love that they know in their heart truly exists. These desires, coupled with their idealistic expectations, leave them vulnerable to developing many fears and insecurities. Here are some of the emotional issues they deal with:

- Beliefs about not being worthy of being loved

- Feelings of inadequacy and low self-esteem

- Inability to accept themselves for who they are

- Fear of being alone

- Frustration with not being able to speak up for themselves or not being taken seriously when they do

- Jealousy stemming from seeing other people more loved than they are

- Being emotionally paralyzed when other people hurt their feelings

- Self-directed anger for not listening to and following their intuition

- Fear of being emotionally hurt or taken advantage of

- Unrealistic expectations around relationships

- Creating relationships that are codependent, emotionally destructive, or emotionally abusive

- Fear of not being accepted

- Fear of being controlled

- Disillusionment when a relationship doesn't give them what they need

The Evolutionary Stage of a Relationship That Greens Are Most Attracted To

As with most things, it's difficult to pin Greens down to just one stage, because they're attracted to all of the initial phases. They have fun meeting others because it's adventurous, they like dating because it's exciting and sexually arousing, they enjoy courtship because it focuses on creating a future together, and they love being engaged because it shows others that they really can commit to one person. All of these stages are exhilarating and emotionally stimulating. They involve being totally focused on and preoccupied with each other—everything the Greens desire and need the most. During this time, the rest of the world and its problems seem to no longer exist. They are just two people falling in love and enjoying each other.

The initial stages of developing a relationship are the playful, intimate, bonding, discovering, and personal-growth times. They tantalize and stimulate the Green's active imagination and entice them to come up with new and different ways to show their love.

Romance, passion, intimacy, and sex are at their peak. The communication process is the most productive and effective because there's the willingness to listen and be fully engaged in conversations. It's when "I love you" flows freely and is more than just a greeting or farewell, and Greens get the verbal reassurance they need in order to feel loved. These stages are especially appealing because they support the sharing of emotions and dreams, and encourage both people to open themselves up to each other, thus revealing insecurities, fears, and their emotional vulnerabilities.

It should be noted that in querying the Greens, there were a disproportionate number of respondents who said that while they enjoyed these initial stages, they don't remember ever thinking about whether they'd grow old with the person they were pursuing. Most of them agreed that they weren't looking that far ahead. They were more interested in living in the moment and enjoying the process than worrying about whether this was the right person. When asked how they knew if someone was the right one, all of them said that they just felt it in their hearts. This was certainly a sharp contrast from the other three colors who determined very early on in these stages whether the person they were pursuing was someone they could spend the rest of their lives with.

The Evolutionary Stage of a Relationship
That's the Most Difficult for a Green

The stage the Greens express the most emotional difficulty settling into is growing together as a couple, although the initial part of this stage isn't a problem. At the beginning of this phase, there's still the element of excitement in setting up a home and learning to live together, and their infatuation is still going strong. The focus is on the relationship and preserving fun and excitement, not on the demands of life. At this point, there's a lot of give and take, along with a willingness to set aside the individual's needs to fulfill the needs of the couple. Setting boundaries about unacceptable behavior and the need for time alone aren't issues yet.

However, when this stage reaches the point where the honeymoon is over, Greens begin to experience a sense of letdown as they realize that their "perfect" mate isn't really perfect, and the love that they thought would spare them from dealing with life's challenges won't actually do so. It's in this part of growing together as a couple that the Greens experience the greatest feelings of disappointment, frustration, and resentment, and begin to question why they were so quick to jump into a relationship.

Seemingly overnight, they find themselves no longer the center of attention. The fatigue and stress that come from trying to juggle a relationship with the demands of life begin to take a toll on their desire for romance, passion, and even sex. The relationship becomes repetitive, and the routine of living together causes the promises of love to wane. Greens start asking themselves, *Is this all there is?*

This is a pivotal time for Greens, and the decisions they make at this point ultimately determine whether the union will last, or if they'll go outside of the relationship to get the attention they need. It's in this phase where Greens will start trying to change and mold their mate into the idealistic image they have in their head.

The difficulties associated with this stage can be overcome if Greens work at remembering why they chose their mate in the first place, and if they can focus on the positive rather than the negative, which is what they always suggest that other people do. It also helps for them to express their emotional needs without creating a confrontation, to spend quality time with their partner, and to enjoy sharing the pleasures of the body (more than just perfunctory sexual activity before falling asleep). If growing together as a couple is the goal, it's important that the spiritual and emotional intimacy needs of the Green are met, and their hearts are replenished with the energy of love each day.

Overview of the Green Personality	
Basic needs:	• Close personal relationships • Creative expression • Finding meaning in life • Freedom to be their unique self
Emotional needs:	• Attention and acceptance • Harmonious and conflict-free environments • Affection • Expression of feelings
Key strengths:	• Creative and intuitive • Go-with-the-flow attitude • Flexible and spontaneous • Optimistic and hopeful
Key weaknesses:	• Gullible and naive • Overly sensitive • Fickle and flighty • Managing time
Primary fear:	• Being alone
Attracted to people who are:	• Fun, playful, and like to laugh • Open to new experiences, adventurous, and enjoy taking risks
Dislike people who are:	• Controlling and domineering • Critical and judgmental • Unwilling to listen
Relationship expectations:	• To be the center of attention • Openness to share their feelings (both positive and negative) • Verbal reassurance
Value in a relationship:	• Spiritual and emotional intimacy and togetherness
Room for improvement:	• Less self-absorbed • Organizational skills • Managing emotional volatility

Overview of the Green Personality, cont'd.	
Annoyances:	• Being treated impersonally
Causes of stress:	• Relationship problems
	• Deadlines
Relationship challenge:	• Managing their idealistic nature
	• Not trying to change their mate into who they want them to be

Hot Tips for Dealing with Greens	
Love	You can never say "I love you" or tell them why you love them too many times. They need verbal reassurance to know they're okay and that the relationship is still good.
Romance	Romantic gestures speak a thousand words. Do unexpected and out-of-the-ordinary things, because they love surprises.
Passion	Do things that make them feel like they're the center of attention. Kiss them all over and whisper sweet endearments in their ear. Call them by their favorite pet names.
Sex	Do something new to break the routine. Try a new toy or position or a location other than the bed.
Communication	Spend a leisurely weekend morning lounging and chatting about what happened during the week. Encourage them to share their feelings and ask them what they'd like to do that day. Actively listen to what they're saying and don't become distracted by other things. Never look at the clock or your watch when they're talking.

Helpful Hints for Greens in Dealing with Other Personality Colors	
Love	Tell them how much you love them and how much you appreciate all they do for you.
Romance	Let your romantic creativity go wild and surprise your mate with something you know they'll enjoy and appreciate. Use romance to seduce them.
Passion	Add some spice to foreplay, and keep it going until your mate is fully aroused.
Sex	Focus on doing things that you know give your mate sexual satisfaction, and then add something new.
Communication	Avoid emotional discussions before going to bed or making love.

PART III

Working at Love to Make Love Work

CHAPTER NINE

How Can We Stay Belly to Belly When We Can't See Eye to Eye?

I once heard this statement: "Anytime we're involved in a relationship with someone other than ourselves, there's bound to
be dysfunction and the potential for conflict." And I remember
thinking how true it was, but not for the obvious reasons that we
might think of, such as the impact of conditioning, societal factors, or even the influence that our parents' relationship had on us.
Instead, it's true because of differences in personality, which create
many of the misunderstandings, disagreements, and conflict we
experience. If we were to ask any member of a couple—whether
short- or long-term—what their greatest relationship challenge is,
they'd most likely say that it has to be dealing with personality
differences.

The process of developing and sustaining a relationship is seldom smooth sailing. It demands a great deal of time, energy, work,
and the willingness to compromise frequently. It tests our commitment to hang in there when we don't see eye to eye and when
the going gets tough. We must constantly look for ways to improve the communication process, and we learn the importance
of setting healthy boundaries.

Relationships are interesting phenomena because they're binary—that is, they're either good or bad, right or wrong. They're growing and flourishing or deteriorating and dying. There are no gray areas when it comes to describing the quality of our bond with that special someone. Think about it: When was the last time you heard someone describe their relationship as being mediocre?

Instead, we hear people say that their relationship is good— really good—or it's bad. When someone says that it's good, what they actually mean is that it's progressing smoothly and free of conflict. In those happy times, we don't question why it's going well, and we don't think about our personality differences. It's only when the unexpected misunderstandings and disagreements pop up, and the flow of the relationship is interrupted, that we begin to actively search for explanations and look for ways to deal with our differences.

Just how common are relationship problems? A research study conducted in 1992 by McGonagle, Kessler, and Schilling revealed that nearly all married couples reported having some form of unpleasant disagreements at some time, with most admitting to at least three unpleasant disagreements per month. The problem with problems isn't that we have them; it's how we choose to deal with them. We can pretend that they don't exist, ignore how they make us feel, or avoid them altogether in the hopes that they'll magically just go away. Or we can see them as opportunities to open up the lines of communication so that we can better understand each other and find more effective ways to deal with the differences that caused them in the first place. If we really want to know what love is all about, we can look to the area of disagreements and conflict, because true love is the ability to manage problems before they begin to erode the relationship.

The Dynamics of Conflict

As anyone who's ever experienced conflict with their partner knows, it causes major distress and instantly changes the nature of the relationship and how we interact with each other. It puts both people in a defensive posture and tends to bring old emotional hurts to the surface. It creates a whole new myriad of feelings and thoughts, opens the door to criticism and rejection, and challenges our personal beliefs and values. If we look at the word *conflict* and break it down, we begin to understand why it impacts us the way it does. "Con" means an argument or evidence in opposition, and "flict" is derived from the same root as the word *inflict,* which means to strike out or to impose. No wonder we become defensive and experience so much stress and tension.

Conflict is an insidious process that, once activated, seems to take on a life of its own. Its patterns are predictable and consistent: It begins as annoyance, leads to misunderstanding, and if not resolved at this point, evolves into disagreement. What causes conflict is also predictable and consistent. It's predictable because it's always tied to something that's being compromised (which is the motivation behind a person's willingness to engage in the process), and at the same time reveals how much that subject means to them. In other words, people feel conflict over things that are important to them. It's consistent in the sense that there are common triggers that arise in any relationship, no matter what the combination of personality colors. These catalysts are money, sex, communication, values, social activities, friends, and responsibility. And once children are involved, parenting joins the list.

Conflict is primarily a personality issue and occurs when people don't see eye to eye, meaning that they have a different perception of the same situation and different expectations about appropriate behavior. This friction reflects power struggles that are occurring within a relationship, which stem from the need for control. As a matter of fact, the greatest potential for dissonance occurs when we're feeling out of control or overly controlled. Conflict brings personality and compatibility issues to the surface that can even cause us to question our choice of a mate. It discloses our vulnerabilities and need for acceptance and forces us to deal with issues related to abandonment and rejection.

In a conflict situation, one person will take on the role of the aggressor and the other will become the defender. The resolution is determined by each person's willingness to compromise their position or their desire to deal with the issues in a friendly fashion. When conflict is resolved amicably, then an equal-partner relationship will evolve, and power struggles will cease to exist. This kind of bond encourages and supports keeping the lines of communication open so that the relationship can grow and flourish.

On the other hand, when the power struggles continue, then a "parent-child" relationship will evolve. This brings up old emotional wounds, and may cause one person to shut down and withdraw. Worse yet, they may give up trying to make things work. The presence of conflict undermines the communication process and erodes the desire to love and be loved. If left unchecked, a parent-child relationship between two supposed equals could eventually lead to the dissolution of the relationship—which may not necessarily be a negative outcome, especially if one person is continually compromising who they are and is unable to express their feelings, needs, and wants.

Now, let's take a more in-depth look at the different elements of conflict and how each personality color deals and copes with them. When applicable, I'll suggest ways to more effectively resolve conflict before it reaches the point of creating hurt feelings and give some dos and don'ts that work for all personalities. I'll also describe how each color deals with conflict, expresses anger, copes with the stress and tension created by these situations, and uses different forms of power to control others. There will be a list of the warning signs you can look for to help you recognize unresolved issues, as well as a list of what annoys each of the four personality colors.

How Conflict Goes from an Annoyance to a Disagreement

To start trying to understand the dynamics of conflict, we need to look at the three stages it goes through. Each one represents a different kind of compromise, as well as the degree of compromise that a person is feeling. The first phase of conflict is annoyance, and it's here that personality traits begin to surface, since members of each type have their own assumptions about how the other colors should act.

When this stage is triggered, it reveals that one person's expectations aren't being met. They're being forced to compromise their standards about what's acceptable behavior and what isn't, although there's usually very little emotional energy invested in the conflict at this stage. The response to annoyances is to either try to change the person's behavior into what we want it to be, or to simply avoid interaction with them at all. Here are some of the annoyances that spark conflict for each color.

What Causes Conflict to Occur

RED

Wasting time, specifically their time

Not having their needs put first

Being taken advantage of

Losing at anything

Lazy, unproductive behavior

Inequity in responsibilities

Not getting their way

Disagreeing with them

Emotional outbursts

Lengthy explanations

YELLOW

Not having the time to think through a decision

Making them look dumb or stupid

Questioning their decisions

False accusations

Being humiliated in front of other people

Questioning their integrity

Questioning their sense of responsibility

Being accountable for other people's mistakes

Dealing with emotional issues

ORANGE

Being treated impersonally

Insensitivity toward others

Not being able to share feelings

Threatening their security

Being criticized

Not being appreciated

Accusations of being self-centered

Not being supported or helped with chores

GREEN

Not being taken seriously

Being criticized

Being ignored

Jealousy

Being suppressed and controlled

Being told when to do something

Time constraints and restrictions

Being overly managed and directed

The second stage of conflict is misunderstandings. They occur when what we *want* to happen, what we *believe* should happen, and what actually *does* happen aren't the same. This usually occurs because of differing perspectives, meaning that one person doesn't see the situation in the same way the other person sees it, and misunderstandings arise when there's sustained tension created by annoyances. These can range from minor situations where people don't see eye to eye, to major events where emotions begin to enter into the dynamics.

Persistent misunderstandings lead to frustration and can ultimately erode the level of trust in a relationship. They cause one person to question the other's judgment, and force both people to justify their perceptions. This stage takes a lot of mental energy and represents a battle of wills. One person thinks that they're right and the other is wrong, and the goal is to change their opponent's way of thinking so that they're in alignment.

If there's no resolution in the misunderstanding stage, then conflict moves into the final stage: disagreements. It's here that anger enters the process and the emotional tension quickly increases. Both people become more adamant about their positions and less willing to compromise what they're thinking or feeling. Once a conflict escalates to this point, the ability to resolve the problem in an amicable way becomes more difficult, because hurt feelings enter into the dynamics.

Disagreements represent the compromise of values and principles. They're the expression of rejection, and basically tell us that who we are—including our perceptions, what we value, and what we're feeling—are all wrong. We not only have to justify our reaction to the situation, but also have to defend our feelings, the position we're taking, and how we're acting. This is where there are accusations and counter-accusations, which can quickly undermine the quality of the relationship.

This phase brings the real causes and motivations behind what we're feeling to the surface. It exposes our fears, insecurities, and vulnerabilities, bringing up old emotional wounds and resurrecting the baggage created by previous relationships. Persistent disagreements jeopardize the longevity of a relationship, because if they aren't controlled, they lead to an either/or ultimatum—and no one deals with that very well.

In the previous chapters for each of the personality colors, there were lists of their fears, insecurities, and anxieties. It might be helpful to go back and review those lists (both yours and your partner's), because they reveal the true underlying causes of conflict in our relationships. It's also helpful to become aware of the warning signs that alert us to unresolved issues. If we can learn to deal with the problems when they first arise, then we have a greater chance of preventing the internal festering of emotions that can ultimately lead to the dissolution of a relationship. Here are some of those warning signs:

- Moodiness
- Silence
- Aggression
- Antagonistic behavior
- Sarcastic comments
- Crying
- Lack of cooperation
- Emotional outbursts
- Indifference
- Withdrawal
- Avoidance

Anytime we don't see eye to eye with those we love, the relationship undergoes tension, stress, and strain. Over the course of time, if the differences aren't resolved, they change the way we feel about our partner and how we interact with them. We find it increasingly difficult to communicate without sounding controlling, defensive, or accusatory. Our tolerance for each other's personality idiosyncrasies decreases, what attracted us in the beginning become annoyances, and we're more judgmental and less receptive to helping each other or trying to solve the problems. Persistent conflict eventually changes our behavior and our willingness to express what we're feeling in a calm and civilized manner. Instead, we express ourselves primarily through anger, which certainly doesn't keep the lines of communication open.

Here's some information that may be helpful in determining how to deal with conflict before it gets to the point of hurt feelings:

Common Conflict Behavior for Each Personality Color	
RED	**YELLOW**
Becomes impatient, abrupt, and argumentative	Becomes tactless, argumentative, and aggressive
Becomes reactive, excitable, and angers easily	Distances themself from their partner
Becomes controlling and demanding	Assumes intellectual superiority over others
Attacks others personally	Challenges thinking and logic
Micromanages people	Displays emotional indifference
ORANGE	**GREEN**
Begins avoiding and accommodating others	Withdraws from interacting with their partner
Worries, frets, and reacts emotionally	Becomes emotionally immobilized
Becomes antagonistic and makes sarcastic comments	Suppresses their feelings
Holds in emotions until the boiling point, then lets loose	Loses objectivity
Becomes emotionally controlling and manipulating	Becomes submissive and blames themself for everything that happens

How Anger Is Expressed When Conflict Occurs

RED

Becomes more forceful

Raises their voice and uses aggressive language

Pounds fists, throws things, and becomes physically aggressive or abusive

Becomes tactless and insensitive

Expresses disgust

YELLOW

Becomes nitpicky and splits hairs

Becomes argumentative

Shows open hostility and contempt

Becomes verbose and challenging

Gives a cold, indifferent stare

Expresses lack of trust

ORANGE

Becomes moody or cries

Yells and makes vengeful, hurtful comments

Becomes emotionally exasperated

Has emotional outbursts

Becomes antagonistic and sarcastic

Expresses disappointment

GREEN

Becomes brooding or cries

Becomes bitter and hateful; gives ultimatums

Shuts down and gives up trying

Displays passive-aggressive behavior

Becomes fickle and unresponsive

Expresses disbelief

Disagreements reveal that there are power struggles occurring in the relationship and indicate that neither person is willing to acquiesce to the other, meaning that they're not going to compromise their position or their values and principles. In this stage, both people have taken a firm stance and believe that what they're thinking or feeling is right. When conflict escalates to this point, it means that it's going to take a lot more than "I'm sorry" to get the relationship flowing smoothly again.

Using power to get what we want is a natural part of our human nature, and we learn at a very early age how to do so. It can be obvious and done blatantly, or it can be subtle and covert. Our motivation may be conscious, meaning that we're fully aware of why and how we're using it; or it can be subconscious, motivated by fears and emotional insecurities. The expression of power can take on many forms: It can be used to intimidate, manipulate, coerce, seduce, influence, protect, control, silence, change minds, comfort, inspire, and motivate. Each personality color is most comfortable using a different form of power to see that their basic needs are met.

Forms of Power Used by Each Personality Color	
RED	**YELLOW**
Control	Superiority
Fear	Knowledge
Retribution	Intimidation
Rejection	Mental manipulation
Physical intimidation	Involvement
ORANGE	**GREEN**
Emotional manipulation	Seduction
Silence	Tears
Blame	Submissiveness
Assertiveness	Guilt
Guilt	Helplessness

Common Conflict Issues

All relationships—no matter how much the two people love each other—are susceptible to issues that have a high probability of creating tension, frustration, and stress. As I mentioned, these common denominators of most conflicts include money, sex, communication, values, social activities, friends, and responsibility. (We're going to leave parenting issues for another book.) Now, add the element of personality differences on top of all this, and it becomes clear why so many couples have a difficult time finding resolutions that will work or that are mutually satisfying.

Until resolved, whenever any of these issues surface, they set off an emotional reaction that instantly changes how we interact and communicate with each other. We become angry, assertive, and defensive; feel compromised; and probably dig in our heels and prepare for the worst. Eventually, these issues and the behaviors associated with them will eat away at the love we have for each other and will create emotional wounds that are difficult to heal. There is hope, however, because the more we understand how we differ from each other, the easier it will be for us to learn how to put ourselves in our partner's shoes. Only then can we see that our mate isn't really trying to make our life miserable—it's just that they don't see things in the same way we do.

The benefits that come from understanding personality are many. And when it comes to conflict and the impact that it has on our relationships, this knowledge can be life altering. Being able to see the issues from our partner's perspective offers us the opportunity to gain a new appreciation for what they bring to the union. It helps calm the troubled waters created by conflict so that we can get back to smooth sailing, and it defuses the strong emotional reactions that could be disastrous to the longevity of the partnership.

Will understanding make the issues go away? Probably not, because they're a part of life, but it *will* change them—they'll become more manageable. Let's take a closer look at each of these common conflict issues and see how each personality color perceives and deals with them.

Money

Other than sex, money carries the most potential for disagreements. This subject triggers strong emotional reactions and brings to the surface many of the fears and insecurities that we carry deep inside. It's also where the need for power and control enters into the love relationship, and where personality differences determine the outcome.

Will this problem be minor or major? When it comes to money, no one wants to be told how to spend or manage it, or that they're handling it incorrectly. Finances are personal and represent different things to each of the personality colors. When this becomes a source of conflict, it seems to bring out the worst in every color.

How we feel about money and manage it can often send mixed messages. In the initial stages of a relationship, there's a tendency to be freer in how we spend. This is because we're usually using money as a means of trying to impress the person we're pursuing. However, in doing so, we're creating expectations and setting a precedent that the other person will use to determine whether we're compatible in this area. If both people still share the same financial perspectives after the excitement and newness of the relationship wears off, then there's a good chance that the initial expectations will remain constant, and money won't become a source of disagreements.

On the other hand, if the initial expectations change as the relationship matures, money can—and usually will—become a major source of disappointment. It can become the impetus behind many heated disagreements. When this occurs, there's a good chance that what we're dealing with are personality differences and their influence on perceptions of money and financial management.

— Money, to the **Red** personality, represents power and status. It reflects their level of success and is a measurement of how good they are at what they do. They use it to impress others, to buy love, and to gain power. As far as Reds are concerned, you either have money or you don't.

Financial success offers Reds the stability they need and makes it possible for them to provide the basic necessities for those they love. This color is conservative when it comes to money and is adamant about controlling its flow. They tend to be frugal and believe in budgeting. They're savers, socking away funds for a rainy day, their retirement, and any financial surprises. When Reds decide to make a major purchase, they're always looking for a good deal and can be aggressive negotiators.

It's not unlike them to challenge someone on this subject and be forthright in telling others what they expect or what they think something is worth. Reds fear that someone will take advantage of them. They'll only put their money into ventures where there are minimal risks—investments that have a proven track record of financial success and that they think are a safe bet. Their perception of money matches the view they have of themselves: conservative and practical.

— Money, to the **Orange**, represents security. They, too, are savers and conservative when it comes to spending, and they're not inclined to buy frivolous, self-indulgent items. Instead, they'd rather buy a house or things that their family needs, or save it for their children's education or a family vacation. Oranges are worriers by nature, and money is a main source of their anxiety. It's also a main source of the guilt they feel, especially if they spend it on themselves.

While not as controlling as the Reds, Oranges generally have a realistic view of where they are financially and are aware of what they can spend and what they can't. They'll also invest, but they'll usually rely on someone else's financial expertise to help them minimize the potential for investing it poorly. The loss of money creates a tremendous amount of stress for them and instantly brings their insecurities and fears of scarcity to the surface.

When they do feel financially secure, Oranges are generous in supporting the causes they believe in and like to help others. They'll contribute money to their church, community services, and other organizations where they have a strong, heartfelt connection. Oranges think that money is best used in serving humanity and giving to those who are less fortunate.

— Money represents independence to the **Yellow** and offers them the freedom to do what they want. It's a resource that they use to add to the fullness of life. It liberates them, letting them do things that make sense to them, rather than having to conform to the rules of life. Yellows are always looking for ways to leverage their money so that it can give them the quality of life they want without having to give up their autonomy.

They, too, are financially conservative in some ways, meaning that they believe in saving and investing. However, they're not as conservative when it comes to investments. They'll take more risks and will include start-ups in their investment portfolios, as well as organizations with freethinkers at the helm. Yellows are the consummate researchers. If they're going to invest in something that isn't a sure thing, they'll look into the company, evaluate the competitors, and find out as much as they can about the people in charge. If they're going to buy something other than basic necessities or maintenance items, they'll spend an inordinate amount of time researching it, just to ensure that their decision is a good one.

Money isn't emotional for the Yellow, so they deal with it in a straightforward manner. They see it as something to be used and maximized—as a means, not an end.

— To the **Green**, money represents the freedom to spend what they want and go wherever they please. They can be savers if they feel that it's important, but they'd prefer to spend their money and live in the now, rather than put it aside for a rainy day. They want to enjoy the fun associated with financial success, such as fulfilling lifelong dreams: buying that impractical car they've always wanted, traveling to exotic places, going on cruises, and sharing it with people they like.

Greens aren't driven by the need for stability, so money isn't a motivator for them to stay in a job that they don't enjoy. They'd rather move from job to job and improve their chances of creating greater wealth than staying stuck somewhere that isn't exciting. Greens like to experience new things, and having money gives them the freedom to change where they live, their jobs, and even their relationships. They value money for opening up a world of endless possibilities. They use it to attend workshops, classes, and conferences that will help them learn more about who they are and teach them how to improve the quality of their relationships.

Their financial planning tends to be more short term, and when they do invest, it's more on an emotional basis rather than out of practicality. They want to put money into companies that offer innovative ways to serve humankind or are interested in saving the environment, rather than corporations that offer solid returns. They want to be a part of things that are new, innovative, and off the beaten path.

Greens are prone to making impulsive purchases, even if they don't have the money to do so. Their attitude is that if they put money out into the universe, more will manifest for them. They want instant gratification, and are usually unwilling to wait until they can save enough for that special treat. They're not known for their patience. Greens are risk takers and may gamble occasionally. Generally, they have a difficult time with money management and knowing where their funds have gone.

Here are some general dos and don'ts about how to deal with money that are applicable to all of the personality colors:

- When money becomes the source of disagreement, **do** identify what the real issue is. Is it spending patterns, money management, impulsiveness, compulsiveness, or balancing the checkbook? Without knowing what the real problem is, it's difficult to find the best solution.

- If you can't come to some mutual understanding, **do** open up three checking accounts: yours, theirs, and one that you both contribute to for covering the basic living expenses.

- **Do** set aside discretionary money for spontaneous and fun spending. Allocate the funds as yours, theirs, and things to do together.

- Early on in the relationship, **do** create a financial team. Determine who's going to handle and manage the money. **Don't** assume that gender roles should drive these decisions.

- **Don't** avoid making each other accountable for every penny spent.

- **Don't** plan only for the present. Agree on an amount that's going to be saved every month.

- **Don't** be sneaky about spending money and try to hide what you buy. Worse yet, **don't** lie about money.

- **Don't** use credit cards if you have a tendency to be impulsive or compulsive.

Sex

Sex is an integral part of what makes a relationship loving instead of fraught with problems and contentious interactions. It's a critical factor in determining the quality of affection that two people share with each other, and strongly impacts the longevity of a relationship. When asked about their sex life, a couple will usually describe it as wonderful, or admit there's definitely room for improvement.

Sex causes the emotions to run high, and the feedback we receive on our sexual performance is directly tied to our ego. When we're told that we're good in bed, we feel good about ourselves; and conversely, when we're criticized for our performance, our ego becomes hurt, as do our feelings. Sex brings issues about power and control to the surface and reveals our vulnerabilities. It seems to come with its own set of hidden agendas and reveals emotional baggage from early sexual experiences, recent relationships, our parents, and religious and social conditioning.

In exploring this subject from the perspective of conflict, we can't just focus on what gives each personality color physical pleasure. We must examine what gives the colors the sexual satisfaction they need in order to feel good about themselves and their relationship. So what affects sexual satisfaction? The answer includes sexual attitude, frequency, aggression, passivity, communication, and incompatibility.

When two people share similar needs, they'll generally feel good about their sex life and relationship, and will express sexual satisfaction. If, on the other hand, there are differences in their needs, it will not only be difficult for them to enjoy the pleasures of a healthy sex life, it will be tough for them to keep their relationship from withering and dying—or from seeking the satisfaction they need with someone other than their mate.

Please don't be misled into believing that understanding personality will eliminate all the problems that you may be experiencing with sex. However, this knowledge *can* offer insights into how each color approaches the subject and what they need in order to be sexually satisfied. At its best, it can provide a nonthreatening communication platform where the two of you can openly and safely discuss your feelings. It can heighten your awareness of what your partner needs in order to feel sexually good about themself, and help you make your relationship more pleasurable.

Remember that sex is complicated, and to approach it stereotypically would be irresponsible. The blending of different personality colors in this area takes understanding, patience, tenderness, cooperation, and emotional sensitivity. It requires a willingness to keep the communication lines open, and a concerted effort on both sides to embrace the uniqueness that each person brings to the relationship. In doing so, many of the frustrations and hurt feelings around sex can be managed.

Sexual Needs by Personality Color

RED

Searching for physical pleasure

Sex starts with the physical sensations

Wants sex regularly so that it can serve as a biological release

Wants physical contact

Wants admiration

Looks for what's familiar

Sexually aggressive

Sex is the ultimate expression of control

When sex is over, it's over—there's no lingering in the afterglow

Needs to hear "I need you"

May not respond sexually if certain familiar foreplay isn't followed

YELLOW

Searching for self-acceptance

Sex starts between the ears, goes to the imagination, and then moves to physical sensations

Wants sex to be mutual so that it doesn't become an emotional or manipulation issue

Wants sensual pleasure

Wants respect

Looks for something different

Sexually sensitive

Sex is the ultimate expression of commitment

When sex is over, this color relives it in their head

Needs to hear "You're good"

May not respond unless the mind is focused on sex

ORANGE

Searching for security

Sex starts emotionally and moves to physical sensations

Wants sex to be meaningful

Wants an emotional bond

Looks for expressions of love

Sexually passive-aggressive

Sex is the ultimate expression of caring

When sex is over, this color enjoys talking about it

Needs to hear "I appreciate you"

May not respond sexually if emotionally distressed

GREEN

Searching for spiritual and emotional connection

Sex starts in the imagination and moves to physical sensations

Wants sex to be fun

Wants variety

Looks for new possibilities

Sexually aggressive and experimental

Sex is the ultimate expression of selflessness

When sex is over, this color revels in the afterglow

Needs to hear "I love you"

May not respond sexually if feeling controlled

Values

The values we form in life about what's important to us are created by a combination of both personality characteristics (what we're taught), and personality traits (what's inherent). These beliefs act as our code of conduct and create the expectations we have of ourselves and others. It's unfortunate that in the initial stages of developing a relationship, we never seem to get around to sharing our values. Instead, we tend to wait and bring them up only after we've made a commitment or even moved on to growing together as a couple.

Depending on the value we place on our word and the strength of our bond with our partner, we may find ourselves spending our lives with someone who doesn't share the same values. The more these beliefs differ, the more difficult it will be to create a relationship built on mutual trust and respect, and the more challenges we'll have in finding mutually satisfying conflict resolutions.

Values include the expectations that we have of ourselves and those we love. They reflect what's important to us: children, family, religion, friends, work, community involvement, and play. They determine our attitudes toward money and how willing we are to spend it on the things we enjoy. They affect our attitude toward employment and our work ethic. Do we live to work, or work to live? Do we expect our partner to share in the financial responsibilities or take care of the family? They influence our need for structure and organization—or the lack thereof. Values determine the importance of love, and contribute significantly to our perceptions of it.

— **Reds** value work and expect others to carry their weight by contributing financially. Their time is very important to them. They like their environment to be orderly and predictable. They treasure family and tradition, and the responsibility of providing for those they love. Reds want consistency and don't care for change or surprises. They need to be financially comfortable and secure; they look forward to the day when they can retire and spend time doing whatever they want. They long for a mate and family who will put their needs first.

— **Oranges** value people and relationships. They need a supportive, emotionally nurturing environment where sharing feelings is encouraged. Children and family are important to Oranges, and doing things as a family adds to the quality of their lives. They value being appreciated for the things that they do for their loved ones, and want to make people happy. The needs of those they love come first, and everything else is secondary. They believe that money is meant to give their families the things that will add to the quality of their lives; it also should be used to help others. They value social activities and giving back to the community.

— **Yellows** value their minds, intelligence, reasoning, and analytical thinking, as well as their freedom, independence, and autonomy. Their capacity to share their knowledge and problem-solving capabilities is important to them, too. They treasure truth, trust, and respect. They pride themselves on their ability to minimize potential problems that could create stress and distress for those they love or are responsible for. Yellows value strong ethics, integrity, and morality. They hold relationships in high esteem where their partner is intelligent, emotionally secure, and stable. They also prize discretionary time.

— **Greens** value friendships, camaraderie, fun, play, and experiencing new things. Spontaneity, unstructured time, freedom, and their uniqueness are important to them. They admire relationships that aren't controlling and where power struggles aren't an issue, and desire conflict-free environments. Greens value learning and sharing their knowledge, along with their creativity, emotions, and intuition. Compassion, tenderness, gentleness, and happiness are all high on their list of key attributes. They find flurries of activity and being with similar personalities rewarding. This color values change and desires the lack of routine and monotony.

In relationships where there's a difference in values, here are some dos and don'ts:

- **Do** be sensitive to each other's feelings. Discuss the differences in values in a nonemotional way. Remember that the objective here is finding ways to live with these variations, not to change each other's values.

- **Do** seek outside professional help if the differences in values are becoming a major source of contention and conflict. It's best to do this before they begin to undermine the love you have for each other and the quality of your relationship.

- **Do** be truthful and upfront if you're unwilling to change a value. **Do** explain the reasons instead of forcing your partner to guess.

- **Don't** try to change your mate's values. **Do** accept and honor them, and look for the positive contributions they make to the relationship.

- **Don't** be critical and judgmental, and don't embarrass your partner in public by discussing your differences in values.

- **Don't** ask other people, such as family members and friends, for their advice on how to deal with your differences. Chances are that they may share the same values, especially if they're the same personality color as you and have been influenced by the same external conditioning.

Social Activities

Another area of potential conflict is social activities—the need for them, determining what activities to get involved in, and deciding who in the relationship is going to be responsible for managing the social calendar. While this subject may not result in major, relationship-threatening disagreements, it certainly can be a source of many misunderstandings that result in couples doing things separately.

If two people share the same personality type, social activities usually won't be a source of contention. It's only when there are differences in personality colors that problems may arise. There's another factor that should be considered when exploring the subject of social activities: introversion and extroversion. It's difficult enough when mates don't share the same personality color without this contrast added into the mix. It's no wonder why misunderstandings often occur in social settings.

Extroverts, by nature, thrive on being around people and participating in social activities. They love being social, experiencing new things with friends, going to parties, and attending activities and events. Being around others—even large groups—energizes them and recharges their social batteries. People are their main source of fun.

Introverts, on the other hand, may dislike going to parties and being around crowds, especially if they don't know the people or have anything in common with them. They'd rather stay at home or participate in low-energy activities, such as socializing with close friends with whom they share common interests. If forced to participate in extroverted activities, they feel exhausted and drained of energy.

Setting aside the factors of introversion and extroversion, here's how the four personality colors view socializing:

— Social activities must serve a purpose for the **Reds**—create or solidify business relationships, satisfy family or business obligations, or be focused on recreational interests. They like to know well in advance what's on the social calendar because they don't like surprises. They prefer to plan what's going to take place and control how much time will be allocated to those activities. They don't like being involved in open-ended events or anything where they don't know the agenda. They prefer having things done their way.

— Social activities must give **Oranges** the warm feelings they need in order to justify the time and energy taken away from their family. They like good food and conversation and sharing their homes with friends and family members. They enjoy attending church and neighborhood events, and getting involved in organizations where being social is the primary objective. This color is organized and skilled at handling the social calendar and takes pleasure in planning get-togethers. They do enjoy their social calendar being full, but not to the point that they don't have any quality time to spend with their family.

— Social activities must appeal to the **Yellows'** interests and challenge their minds. While not really antisocial, they may appear this way because they'd rather stay at home or work than to have to participate in events that involve small talk or being with people they don't know—or with whom they have nothing in common. Yellows enjoy gatherings with close friends and ones where the conversations are thought provoking and mentally stimulating. They want to be involved in activities that challenge them and test their skills and where they can compete against themselves. It's probably best for the Yellow to turn their social calendar over to someone who has a need for fun and being around others. Otherwise, they may tend to work all the time.

— Social activities must be fun for **Greens** and feed their need to play. They enjoy being socially active and tend to overschedule. This color doesn't need a reason to be with people, and being social doesn't have to serve a purpose. They like to initiate new ways to draw people together and to create theme parties. Greens enjoy events where there are lots of people expressing their excitement and having fun, such as ball games, concerts, parties, conferences, and conventions. They'll use any excuse to get together and do things with their friends and prefer leaving their schedules open so that they can be flexible if something better comes along. They'd rather be footloose and fancy-free than tied down to a calendar or committed to something that might be boring. Even introverted Greens can tolerate being around large groups of people just because it's fun.

If you're in a relationship where you and your partner are different personality colors *and* different in introversion and extroversion, the best way to deal with your social-activities issues is to talk about them before they become a problem. Be honest and forthright in telling each other what you need and want socially. Then discuss how you can balance each other's needs and find a compromise that will keep you both socially satisfied.

Friends

Friendships, especially those outside the relationship, may be a major catalyst for stress and tension and can become the source of many disagreements. Our friends basically reflect who we are and personify our perception of ourselves. They make us feel good about ourselves and offer us the support and comfort we need when the going gets tough—which we may not be able to get from our mate.

In evaluating this area, it's interesting to note that when we create our friendships, we tend to choose people who are similar to us, meaning that they share our same personality color, interests, social needs, and values. Yet when it comes to creating a love relationship, we don't necessarily follow those same guidelines. Instead, there's a tendency to be attracted to our opposites—who in most cases *aren't* the people we'd seek as friends.

There's a lot of emotion and ego associated with how we feel about our friends, and when someone raises questions about these people, all of the personality colors will immediately become defensive and dig in their heels. These disagreements are really bringing power and control issues within the relationship to the surface, along with our fears and insecurities. When our mate questions our friends or disapproves of them, what we hear and feel is criticism of our judgment and values and that there's an element of distrust.

While no one likes to have their choices and beliefs challenged, it's the implied suspicion that leads to hurt feelings and that can ultimately erode the love we have for each other. Whenever the subject of friends is being discussed, it must be done with a heightened sensitivity to each other's feelings, and a careful monitoring of the words and tones of voice that we use as we disclose our issues regarding those friends. Without that sensitivity, any requests can sound like ultimatums, which in turn makes it more difficult to find solutions that can give both people what they need.

As a couple, it's beneficial to have "couple" friends (whom both partners like) and "separate" friends (who are closer to one person or the other), because each type is valuable in teaching us how to appreciate our love relationship. Sharing time with couple friends creates the opportunity for us to function as a team, and reminds us to appreciate the things that we each contribute to that joint effort.

Separate friends create the opportunity for us to express our individuality and offer us relationships where we don't have to work as hard to find similarities. The challenge, however, is finding a comfortable balance between the time we spend with these people and the time we spend with our mate. Separate friends need to enhance our love relationship, not distract from it. If they happen to be of the opposite sex, we must be careful not to make our partner feel insecure or emotionally inadequate by turning to these companions rather than our mate for comfort.

Another challenge with separate friends of the opposite sex is that their presence reveals insecurities related to jealousy, fear of abandonment, and betrayal. This again requires a heightened sensitivity. It means being careful not to slip into a romantic or sexual relationship with those friends, or displaying behavior that would cause your mate to question the love you have for them. It all comes back to the element of trust, and if distrust surfaces, it creates a no-win situation.

— **Reds** tend to create friendships with bosses, co-workers, and other business associates. Much of the time that they share with their friends is focused on developing and strengthening their work relationships. As with social activities, friendships must serve a purpose for Reds. Their friendships can be superficial and without emotional connections, or they can be strongly emotional and deeply rooted.

When a friendship has a strong bond, it's usually because it was created under some adverse condition, such as being in the military; struggling to climb the corporate ladder; or dealing with the death of a mate, the loss of a job, or the breakup of a relationship. Reds want companions who share similar interests. They're not receptive to their mate having separate friends, especially if those friends' needs come first.

— **Oranges** want a variety of friends, including ones from church and community organizations, co-workers, and neighbors. They look for good, close comrades and prefer couple friends, because they can share these connections with their mate. When they do have separate friends, Oranges will tend to spend time with them only when it won't take away from the needs of their family. They want friendships that encourage and support the expression of feelings, and where sharing time together is meaningful.

— **Yellows** are more interested in having a few close confidants than a large social circle. While they enjoy the company of couple friends, they really desire to have one best friend. They want someone whom they can confide in and share quality time with—someone who's a close companion as well as a "good-times" friend. In seeking out a love relationship, the Yellow will look for that bond with their mate. As a rule, if they're lucky enough to find a partner who becomes their best friend, they won't have any need for independent socializing. As a matter of fact, separate friendships distract from the quality of their relationship rather than enhance it.

For Yellows, friendships create deep and meaningful connections. They tend to be lifelong, even though they may not see those people regularly. No matter how many years pass between get-togethers, when the Yellow is reunited with their friends, it's as if they've never been separated. This color enjoys being around intellectually challenging people with whom they can share opinions, banter, and spar.

— **Greens** love having lots of friends: close pals, best buddies, mere acquaintances, and even superficial hangers-on. They want harmonious friendships where there are no hidden motives for power or the need to control. They like to create alliances with people who aren't demanding or quick to judge their changeability. Greens can be fickle, meaning that they can be inseparable with someone one minute, and in the next moment move on to someone else. They tend to put their friends' wishes first and everyone else's second. They place a lot of value on their social circle and need it in order to feel good about themselves. They want to share experiences where just being together is fun.

If you're experiencing friendship issues in your relationship, here are some dos and don'ts:

- If you have issues with your mate's friends, **do** discuss them rather than holding your feelings inside. The suppression of feelings can lead to resentment.

- **Do** schedule time with couple friends and with separate friends. Then **do** set aside time for just the two of you to be alone.

- **Do** be truthful in setting boundaries as far as what's acceptable behavior with friends and what isn't.

- If you're feeling uncomfortable with your mate's friends, **do** ask yourself if the people involved are really the problem, or if you're dealing with your own insecurities.

- If your partner is planning to spend time with their friends, **do** use that opportunity to socialize on your own.

- **Don't** give ultimatums when it comes to friends—you might not like the outcome.

- **Don't** put your mate in the position of defending their friends, and **don't** question what they do when they're all out together.

- **Don't** tell your mate what friends they can and can't have.

- **Don't** ever express the negative feelings you have about your mate's friends directly to those individuals. If you do, you'll embarrass and humiliate your mate and put them in an untenable situation.

Responsibility

The final area of conflict we'll discuss in this chapter is the issue of responsibility. Because of its broad implications, we'll look at it in the context of actions rather than who we are (that is, passing judgment). Judging others isn't the intent of this book because all that does is open the doors for blame and criticism, and it focuses negatively on differences rather than on positive contributions. What we'll be exploring here is how each of the personality colors perceives this topic, and the expectations they have around sharing it.

Conflict around responsibility only tends to surface when someone perceives an imbalance, meaning that one person thinks or feels that they're carrying more of the burden for making things happen than their mate is. This issue tends to flare up around money, sex, communication, values, social activities, and friends—as well as time, chores, family obligations, work duties, parental roles, and even emotional obligations to those we love.

Let's face it, no one wants to be in any situation—let alone a romantic partnership—where they feel misused or abused. Aren't relationships and the burden for making them work a team effort? Isn't sharing responsibility supposed to be fair and equitable? Over and over again in my love workshops, I hear complaints about feeling taken advantage of and not being appreciated.

When I hear these comments, my recommendation is always the same: If responsibility becomes a point of contention, deal with it before the power and control issues surface and emotions flare. The objective of a truly loving relationship is to keep the burden balanced. After all, it's the only way to prevent frustration, resentment, and anger from creeping in and festering to the point where they undermine the affection and respect that we have for each other.

The expectations we have as far as responsibility is concerned are directly influenced by our perceptions of it, and which are determined by the values established by our personality color. Values and responsibility are largely synonymous, and both carry strong emotional reactions. Now this isn't to imply that conditioning and external factors don't affect how we express those assumptions, because they do. It's just that they don't *create* responsibility expectations—the personality does.

As discussed earlier, values reflect the core of who we are and create the principles by which we live our lives. In love relationships where interactions aren't motivated by the need for power and control, issues related to responsibility seldom arise. This is because both people are sensitive to maintaining a balance as far as who does what and how much each one does. And if for any reason one person is unable to fulfill their responsibilities, then the other assumes them without feeling taken advantage of—because they see themselves as a team. When a couple shares in the responsibilities, they actually strengthen their partnership by creating feelings of mutual respect.

Problems revolving around responsibility occur most often when there are differences in personality colors. Here's a brief overview of how each color views the subject and the expectations they have of their mate:

— **Reds** take responsibility very seriously and allow that to drive their behavior. They see it as their duty to provide the basic needs for their families, such as food, shelter, and clothing. Consequently, they automatically assume the burden of making and managing the money. In doing so, they can ensure that those they love will have what they want and need, and will be safe and secure.

Reds equate responsibility with working for what they want and need. They have no tolerance for people who aren't willing to be accountable for their actions, and they can't understand how someone could take from another person and not be willing to give back in some way. Not contributing is unacceptable behavior in their book. They're judgmental and critical of others when it comes to this topic.

Reds expect their mate to share in the responsibilities of running a household, which can include contributing financially or performing the tasks necessary for maintaining a comfortable, orderly quality of life. When their partner assumes their share of the household chores, the Red can focus all of their attention on work and making money.

— **Oranges** view it as their responsibility to take care of the personal and emotional needs of those they love. This means taking on errands and tasks so that their mate doesn't have to. They put the needs of their family before their own. Oranges believe it's their duty to provide emotional support, comfort, and encouragement when the burdens of responsibility weigh heavily on their mate. Worrying is their job, and they'll fret about anything and everything.

In return, it's their mate's duty to acknowledge with appreciation all that the Orange does. They expect their partner to be sensitive to their needs and emotionally available when they're having a bad day or a crisis. They expect the other person to listen and share in the responsibility of caring for the family, including helping with the chores—not just providing financial security.

— **Yellows** take responsibility for being the protectors of those they love, and do so by being mentally and physically supportive and available. It's their perceived duty to prevent their mate's problems, and to see that those issues don't recur in the future. This sense of obligation overshadows all of their behavior and personal needs. They see it as their *job* to be responsible.

Yellows won't shy away from conflict or shun their protective duties if they feel that they or their mate are being unfairly attacked. They'll take on whatever role is necessary—provider, protector, caretaker, nurturer, supporter, or consoler—if they think that will prevent emotional problems and conflict from occurring within their relationship.

Yellows expect very little in return from their mate, other than to take on equal responsibility in making the relationship work, and to be understanding. This means minimizing emotional outbursts and distractions, following through on commitments, and valuing each other's time. They expect their partner to be just that—an equal teammate. Yellows become resentful if they feel that their mate isn't doing their fair share. If they see it as their responsibility to work long hours, they expect the other person to be understanding and supportive.

— **Greens** view it as their responsibility to see that those they love are happy. Consequently, it's their job to be cheerful, inspirational, encouraging, and emotionally supportive. They see it as their duty to personify love and to teach others how to love. Responsibility can be burdensome and limiting to the Green, especially if it requires engaging in tasks that are unappealing and repetitive.

They believe that they should be available for their friends if they're in need, even if that means shunning their obligations at home. For Greens, responsibility is a moving target that shifts depending on what they're doing at the time. Rather than being rigid about duties, they want the room to shift them if something different comes along. Greens expect their mate to be supportive and emotionally understanding if they don't follow through on their commitments—yet they can be emotionally rigid and manipulative when their mate behaves that way.

If you're experiencing conflict because of responsibility issues, here are some recommendations on how to deal with them:

- **Do** schedule a discussion about who's responsible for which tasks or actions at a time when emotions aren't flaring.

- If responsibility resentment surfaces, **do** tell your mate what's bothering you before it reaches the level of anger. **Don't** try to calmly communicate what you're feeling when you really want to lash out.

- When discussing responsibility, **do** show your mate the same courtesy, patience, and understanding that you'd show your best friend or a work associate.

- **Don't** attack your mate personally about these issues. **Do** remember that they'll probably feel as if you're insulting their values.

- As difficult as it may be, **don't** put your own needs first. If this becomes a battle of wills, finding an amicable distribution of responsibility will be difficult—if not impossible.

- **Don't** get caught up in a nitpicky, tit-for-tat, heated discussion about gender roles. Times have changed, and so should the perceptions of who does what.

A Parting Thought

Yes, conflict is uncomfortable, undesirable, and emotionally draining—and it certainly tests our love and our willingness to work at making love work. Will understanding personality differences eliminate all strife from our relationships? Certainly not, but what it can do is help us realize that when conflict arises, our partner is probably not trying to make our life miserable. It's just that how they perceive the issues is different from the way we do. Knowing our personality color and that of our mate dramatically changes the nature of conflict and how we interact with each other in those stressful times. Hopefully, it increases our tolerance and helps us find constructive ways to reduce the amount of discord we experience.

As difficult as it may be to accept, conflict is a normal part of personal growth and the development of a relationship. Through this tension, we have the opportunity to let go of any false, idealistic illusions that we may have with respect to what love should be or how we should interact with each other. Conflict brings out feelings, thoughts, attitudes, and beliefs that are the result of what we've been taught rather than what love really is. These struggles reveal our need for power and control; and expose our fears, insecurities, and emotional vulnerabilities so that we can recognize them.

Times of conflict require that we seek new solutions, make changes, and find more effective ways to interact with each other. They teach us how to compromise without feeling compromised, and they open our hearts to the love that supports finding new truths that will be mutually liberating. The bottom line is that conflict forces us to talk and listen.

CHAPTER TEN

I Know You Think You Heard What I Was Saying, but That's Not Necessarily What I Meant

Have you ever been in a conversation with someone and felt like you weren't even speaking the same language? Is getting on the same wavelength with your mate a challenge—to say the least? Or has your partner ever asked how you feel, and you found yourself unsure of how to respond? Did that leave you wondering if it was a trick question—just another way to engage you in a conversation where they could air their feelings about you and your actions? Perhaps you thought they wanted to bring up all the ways that you've hurt their feelings, or what you're not doing right, or what about you is bugging them—and how it has bugged them for a long time. To help understand the impact that our personality has on how we communicate, let's take a quick look at how each of the four personality colors would most likely respond to the question "How do you feel?"

— **Reds'** knee-jerk response to such a question would be literal. They'd say, "With my hands." Now, if you're a Red or a Yellow, that response wouldn't be a problem. It's a straightforward answer to a straightforward question. But if you're an Orange or a Green, that response would hurt your feelings and would most likely escalate into a conflict-charged conversation.

183

— **Oranges'** response would be emotional. They'd see it as sincere outreach and the opportunity to share how they're really feeling, so they'd confide everything in their lives that's causing them to feel they way they do.

— **Yellows** would have to think before responding, because they'd immediately assume that it might be a loaded question. Especially if they hadn't answered it "right" previously, they'd figure that they shouldn't be quick to respond this time. Better yet, they'd decide not to say anything at all in the hopes that the conversation would move on to something else that they're more comfortable in discussing—a subject that's not so charged with emotions. On the other hand, if it was the Yellow asking *you* how *you* feel, they'd be eagerly anticipating you confessing a problem so that they could help you solve it.

— **Greens** see the question "How do you feel?" as just a way of acknowledging your presence—sort of like "Hello," "Hi there," "Glad to see you," or "What's new?" They believe that it's a "positional" question, meaning that it's designed to initiate a conversation. It opens the door to sharing what's going on in your life, expressing what you're doing for fun, and communicating what exciting adventures you've been involved in. This color could also interpret it to mean "How's your relationship and your love life?"

With all this variation, is it any wonder that we get so frustrated with the communication process and have trouble getting on the same wavelength?

Communication: A Common Word, an Ongoing Challenge

We all want to be heard and to receive a response—and even more important, to be understood. The objective of communication is to see that each of these goals is met by creating an equal exchange of both talking and listening. Yet if we were to ask couples if their communication expectations were being met, we might find ourselves having to listen to a long list of complaints. These could include:

- They don't listen.
- All they do is talk.
- They don't care.
- They have no feelings.
- They're too busy thinking about what they're going to say next.
- They just plain don't understand what's being said.

As I said earlier, the most common complaint in love relationships and a major source of conflict is *lack of communication.* However, this doesn't necessarily mean that there's a shortage of words being spoken. Rather, there's a lack of quality and sensitivity accompanying those words. That is, it isn't what we say that's important—it's how we say it. Even the most discussed issues can still remain unclear if someone is saying one thing and the other person is hearing something else.

An ongoing challenge is that as the relationship evolves into commitment and we grow together as a couple, there's a tendency to settle in and not spend as much time talking and listening to each other. Sitting down and sharing what was happening in our lives when we were apart is preempted by the demands of work and family. And unfortunately, as relationships mature, the conversations change from talking about *we* to talking about *me.*

Notice that I just used the word *talking* . . . and that without listening, communication is a one-sided venture. While speaking is effective in expressing whatever's on our mind or getting what we're feeling off our chest—it doesn't necessarily result in a mutually satisfying conversation. But when talking and listening are equally distributed, the expectations we each have about communication are fulfilled. We experience a sense of being in sync with our mate and feel good about meeting on common ground.

This can either make or break the relationship. If we're to keep our love for each other thriving and growing, then we must learn to communicate effectively—and that means using words that our partner can relate to and saying them in a way that they'll understand. It also means *actively listening*, and not allowing our minds to wander off to something else in the middle of a conversation.

Contrary to the myths created by societal conditioning, effective communication isn't just about getting our point across or trying to gain control. It's not intended to be a power struggle, and it certainly it isn't meant to be a contest where one person wins and one loses.

Instead, it's about being open and receptive. It means listening, taking in what we hear, and absorbing it before responding. We need to evaluate what's been said from our mate's perspective, and be open to changing our minds if what we hear makes sense or feels right to us. It means being able to speak each other's language, and to do so without thinking or feeling that we have to compromise our values or who we really are.

Effective communication is arrived at through trial and error, patience, and a continually mindful practice of listening. It requires an acceptance and understanding that this is a dynamic, ever-changing process; and we must pay attention to each of these factors if it's to be effective:

- What we say (verbal)
- How we say it (voice tones)
- What we don't say, but our body language does (nonverbal)
- How we listen (active or passive)
- Acknowledgment that we've received information and understand what's been said (acceptance)

Only when all of these are included can the lines of communication remain open, letting us learn to deal with our differences and appreciate what each person contributes to the relationship. We all crave discussions that are expressed and heard with compassion—that deepen the level of intimacy with our mate and help us weather the stormy times when we don't see eye to eye.

This kind of communication teaches us new things and expands our perception of who we are individually and as a couple.

What's Personality Got to Do with It?

While all communication problems can't be blamed on personality, those basic differences can definitely wreak havoc and undermine the pleasure that we get from our conversations. In trying to understand what personality has to do with it, we have to start by looking at how our inherent neurological hardwiring (traits) affects our decision-making process, because it's here that the breakdown in begins.

There are two ways that we can make choices, and while both are always available, our personality neurology specifically prefers one method over the other. The options are:

1. We can make decisions based on logic.

2. We can make decisions based on emotions (meaning that it must *feel* right before we can move forward with it).

If we go with Option 1, the words that we'll use to communicate our thoughts will be more literal in their meaning and more succinct, and they'll clearly verbalize what we're thinking. This will elicit a logical response. Conversely, if our preference is for Option 2, we'll tend to use metaphorical and symbolic words that aren't as precise; they'll reflect what we're feeling in our heart versus thinking in our head. This will elicit an emotional reaction.

The Red and Yellow personalities make decisions based on logic, while the Oranges and Greens go with their emotions. The trouble begins when these decision-making differences are paired in a couple. As soon as one person speaks, the divergence surfaces; and what's said, heard, meant, and interpreted can leave us feeling like we're total strangers. For example:

— A Yellow tells their Orange mate that they don't want them to take what they're about to say personally. The Orange thinks, *Here we go again with the criticism and judgment. Always Mr./Ms. Perfect.* When the Orange clams up and doesn't respond favorably to the suggestions offered, the Yellow can't understand why their partner doesn't want their help or to listen to their solutions. After all, the Yellow sees themselves as just trying to help.

— A Green tells their Red mate that they're going to run out to the store and will be back in a few minutes. What the Red thinks is: *A few minutes—that's five or six minutes—which is only 300 to 360 seconds. Not long.* If the Red reacts strongly when their partner returns home a couple of hours later, the Green can't understand what the problem is. Time is literal to the Red, but not to the Green.

— An Orange says to their Red mate, "We need to talk." The Red thinks, *Here we go again with the emotional outbursts. I wonder how long this conversation will take this time? They're never happy.*

— In a conflict-charged confrontation, a Green says to their Yellow mate, "I'm out of here," meaning that they've had it with this conversation. They're going to another room or outside—anywhere to get away from this uncomfortable situation. The Yellow thinks, *Out of here? Is it for good or just a little while? Where are they going? Is the relationship over? Will they be back?*

It's a wonder that we ever manage to communicate with each other at all! These examples begin to shed light on why we send and receive mixed messages, and why we don't always get the responses we're looking for.

The burden of responsibility in this process doesn't fall on the other person's shoulders, requiring them to adapt and adjust to our personality neurology. It falls on our shoulders. It's our job to speak their language by using words that they can relate to, and that they can mentally or emotionally decode. If we don't, they truly can't understand what we're saying.

A helpful hint: If you can learn to actively listen to the words your mate uses, you'll discover that they're disclosing their personality neurology to you through those phrases. Then all you have to do is learn to use the same expressions when talking to them. This simple process can drastically reduce the potential for frustration and minimize the conflict that occurs when what's being said isn't interpreted as the speaker intended.

The Problem with Verbal Communication

The verbal aspect of communication relies solely on the use of words to convey thoughts and information, and consequently requires that words be used as a response. This process is inherently impersonal, and its intention is to express needs, opinions, values, expectations, and beliefs. In a conversation where the people involved don't relate to words in the same way, the responses are often unexpected—and they often discourage us from talking anymore.

When the feedback we get isn't what we were expecting, it may catch us off guard. It's the element of surprise that creates the barriers that can take a productive conversation and turn it into a confrontation. "Productive" means that the participants receive the information they're looking for in the way they need it, and there's joint understanding of what was said. When the lines of communication break down, instead of hearing what the other person *meant,* we might come away with these impressions:

REDS ARE:

Overly controlling

Blunt and discourteous

Abrupt

Insensitive

Full of themselves

Always giving orders

Not interested in what anybody else has to say

YELLOWS ARE:

Overly critical

Arrogant

Verbose

Nitpicky

Cold and aloof

Combative

Lecturing

ORANGES ARE:

Overly sensitive

Artificially sweet, meddling, and interfering

Focusing only on problems

Acting as if everything is a problem

Unsure about what they want

Submissive

Not genuine—superficial

GREENS ARE:

Overly personal

Uncommitted

Evasive

Indecisive

Lacking focus

Confused

Unrealistic

A helpful hint: Verbal communication requires being mentally engaged in the process, meaning that we must actively listen to what's being said by paying attention to the exact words being used—nothing more.

A verbal-communication clue: If a person repeatedly uses a version of the word *think* in their conversations—such as "This is what I think" or "Here are my thoughts"—there's a good chance that they're a Red or a Yellow, because their personality neurology requires that they make decisions based on logic and thinking. The Red or Yellow is just providing information in a direct, impersonal manner that's true to their color.

If a person repeatedly uses the word *feel* in their conversations—such as "This is how I feel" or "My feelings are this"—there's a good chance that they're an Orange or a Green, because their personality neurology requires that they make decisions based on emotions and what feels right. The Oranges and Greens are expressing what they're feeling in their heart about the information they're sharing, which is true to their color.

The Problem with Nonverbal Communication

Nonverbal communication, on the other hand, directs our attention more to the subtleties around the words being spoken. It requires that we listen to voice tones and inflections and pay attention to body language. This reveals the hidden messages and motives behind the words. Our emotional sensitivity is heightened so that we're able to discern how a person feels about what they're saying—and how we're feeling about it.

Rather than getting impersonal responses as we do in the verbal process, this type of communication involves reactions, which are sometimes strongly negative ones that we might not be expecting. Again, it's the element of surprise that can put up barriers and cause a breakdown in understanding. However, unlike the blocks in verbal communication (which aren't emotionally charged and merely require that we change the words being used), the nonverbal obstacles are more difficult to overcome because they involve hurt feelings, which are tied to power and control issues in relationships.

Nonverbal communication conveys meaning rapidly, because it provides immediate feedback. Through voice tones and inflections and body language, we're able to read between the lines and discern whether what's being said is true, if the person is sincere, whether they're receptive or unapproachable, interested or disinterested. We don't have to wait for the brain to process the words or depend on the speaker to find the right phrasing. We understand instantly what's being said because we feel it in our body— we either feel calm or stressed.

Here again, personality neurology plays a major role because it immediately distinguishes between the Reds and Yellows (logical) and Oranges and Greens (emotional), revealing how those differences impact a person's ability to read the nonverbal messages.

Because of their neurology, the first two colors aren't as inclined to pay attention to the subtleties, clues, and cues associated with nonverbal interaction. They're more focused on the words being spoken than interpreting the innuendoes behind them. For these individuals, the communication process is an impersonal exchange of information based on what's said, and they only become aware of any nonverbal aspects when the conversation becomes confrontational and stressful. In other words, when they get blindsided by an emotional reaction they didn't expect.

The Oranges and Greens, however, see the communication process as an intimate interpersonal interaction. For them, the verbal part is only a very small portion of the encounter—just a place to begin. The nonverbal aspect has the most value for them because it lets them read between the lines in order to gain a better understanding of what's being said. Consequently, these colors see the exchange of information more as an expression of respect, trust, admiration, caring, empathy, and a myriad of other emotional reactions, rather than an exchange of words.

Their perspective is that effective and productive communication—which means an encounter that meets their emotional needs—must be genuine and sincere and include the expression of feelings. They're less inclined to engage in conversations where the objective is to focus on what's being said. Their perception is that very little communication is actually taking place in those situations, and that it's more about watching someone talk to themselves.

Since the Oranges and Greens instinctively use their emotional neurology to evaluate information and read between the lines, they tend to recall past conversations more accurately. Unlike the Reds and Yellows, who can't remember what was said a few minutes after the fact, the Oranges and Greens can not only tell us what they remember about the discussion, they can relate how they felt at the time, whether it was really a conversation or a lecture, and whether their feelings were hurt in the process. They have the capacity to remember word for word the details that the Reds and Yellows see as mental clutter, which is deleted from their memories shortly after being said.

A helpful hint: Nonverbal communication requires that we participate emotionally in the process, meaning being sensitive to *how* things are being said and paying attention to facial expressions, eye contact, and physical gestures.

A nonverbal-communication clue: Watch a speaker's body language, because it will tell you their personality neurology, as well as how they feel about the communication process. If someone touches their head repeatedly in a conversation, it reveals that they're thinking about what's being said. These gestures can include rubbing their head, wiping their eyes, cleaning their glasses, running their fingers through their hair, or rubbing their face or chin—basically any repetitive movement above the shoulders. Their body language is telling you that there's a good chance that they're a Red or a Yellow, and that their personality neurology places a greater importance on what they're thinking than what they're feeling in their heart.

If someone touches their chest by putting one or both hands on their heart while talking, rubbing their shoulders, patting their chest, or crossing their arms, then there's a good chance that they're Orange or Green. This means that their personality neurology places a greater importance on how they feel in their heart than the thoughts that are going through their head. Their body language reveals that they're making a sincere emotional decision and perceiving the conversation with their heart. They're conveying how they feel—not about the words that are being spoken, but how they feel about you.

The What-Why Phenomenon

There's an interesting phenomenon that takes place in the communication process, and that's how the words *what* and *why* actually evoke diametrically opposed physical changes in the body and strongly influence how we act and react to information, both verbally and nonverbally. Let me explain: Obviously, both words are intended to pose a question, both are seeking clarification of what's been said, and both are requesting additional information. However, they don't evoke the same kind of response. One supports staying calm, and the other sets off the stress alarm.

In many cases, questions that begin with "Why" trigger a strong emotional reaction that sets off the fight-or-flight stress response. These kinds of inquiries put us in a defensive posture and tend to catch us off guard. They make it sound as if our thinking, values, and beliefs are being challenged, and we're being personally attacked. Take a moment and think back to a conversation where someone hit you with a "Why" question (or for that matter, maybe a series of them): "Why did you do that?" "Why weren't you listening?" "Why do you treat people the way you do?"

Isn't it interesting that it was probably difficult for you to respond instantaneously? And when you did answer, you were probably reacting emotionally rather than giving a rational response. "Why" questions are intended to do that to you, because the motivation behind them is to find out how a person is feeling about something. For the Reds and Yellows, such an inquiry can make their blood boil, cause their faces to turn red with anger, and bring out the worst in their personality colors.

On the other hand, Oranges and Greens use this strategy all the time. Contrary to what the Reds and Yellows may think, this isn't done maliciously, but because these questions give them the feedback they need in order to get a clear reading on what's going on. "Why" helps them understand.

"What" questions, however, speak to the logical, analytical part of the brain. They request that a person share what they're thinking or their logical thoughts on the matter. Since these inquiries evoke a measured response rather than an emotional reaction, they're less inclined to create tension and stress in the physical body. Consequently, a person's thinking can remain clear and their body calm.

Again, take a moment and think back to a conversation where "What" questions were asked: "What are your reasons for doing that?" "Can you explain to me what you meant by that statement?" "What can we do to resolve the problem?" Isn't it interesting how easy it was for you to share what was on your mind and how productive the conversation was?

These questions require a clear and concise response. The Reds and Yellows use them to gather the information they need in order to make logical decisions—which they consider the right decisions. These queries make it possible for them to focus impersonally on the exchange of information, not bogging down the communication process with what they view as emotional minutiae.

The Oranges and the Greens see "What" questions as a form of interrogation and lacking the personal sensitivity needed to engage them in the conversation. They perceive them as a form of manipulation that the Reds and Yellows use to try to gain control and emotionally silence them. Consequently, the Oranges and Greens get resentful and feel pressured when asked a series of "What" questions. They tend to hold their breath and pull their shoulders up to their ears, as if trying to tell the Reds and Yellows to get off their back.

Speaking the Language of Color

Getting on the same wavelength doesn't have to be difficult if we understand how each personality color approaches the communication process, and recognize what they need in order to get the information the way they can use it—that is, learn to speak the language of their color. But first let's do a quick review of what we've learned so far in this chapter.

We found that listening for key words in verbal communication will reveal a person's personality neurology—the key words are *think* and *feel*. Next, we learned that in the nonverbal process we can watch body language for specific physical gestures that will tell us about personality—touching the head or the chest. Now, let's take this a step further by learning more about how each color approaches communication, as well as some techniques to help ensure that conversations will be mutually productive. The benefits of this knowledge include:

- Minimizing the potential for misunderstandings and disagreements

- Eliminating unproductive and frustrating conversations that leave both people wondering what happened

- Reducing the amount of tension and stress caused when we can't get on the same wavelength

- Lessening the potential for inaccurate assumptions, which can lead to incorrect decisions

- Communicating with integrity and respect versus power and control

- Keeping the lines of communication open even when conversations are charged with emotions

As I stated earlier, it isn't the responsibility of those we're speaking with to figure out our mode of communication; it's our job to adapt to them. The key lies in our ability to recognize how each personality color processes information, and then to rise above the differences and meet them on common ground. It's also helpful if we keep in mind that what's exciting and mentally stimulating to some colors can be emotionally draining and debilitating to others.

Reds and Yellows see every conversation as an opportunity to gain knowledge, learn, teach, or solve problems. Their prime objective in the communication process is achieving the maximum understanding for both the sender and the receiver. Achieving this goal may mean that they question, play devil's advocate, or take an opposing position just so that they can gain clarity and fully comprehend the issue.

While this isn't a problem for them, it can be frustrating and even anger the Oranges and Greens, because they don't share the same objective. Their goal in the communication process is to share feelings and create conversations that are meaningful, personal, and mutually beneficial—and that lack any hint of conflict. They don't rely on communication to improve something, but rather look at it as means of enjoying being with someone.

How to Speak Red	
DOs	**DON'Ts**
Be clear about what you want to say before you begin.	Don't use words that are emotionally charged or that will elicit an emotional reaction.
State the facts and stick to the point.	Don't ask "Why" questions.
Tell and show them what you're trying to get across (they're auditory and visual).	Don't ask them how they feel about something.
Draw upon past experiences that they're familiar with to make your point.	Don't change the subject mid-sentence and be sure to finish your sentences.
Ask them what they think.	Don't repeat yourself—it's okay for them, but not you.
Always be prepared to support what you're saying.	Don't waste their time exploring ideas or discussing concepts. Come to them when you have something tangible.
Minimize small talk.	Don't skirt around issues. Say it like it is.
Be assertive and self-confident.	Don't put them in a position where they have to defend what they're saying.

How to Speak Orange	
DOs	**DON'Ts**
Begin the conversation on a positive note and express your appreciation.	Don't ask them to do anything that's offensive or that will cause them to be hurtful to others.
Encourage them to talk about their concerns about other people.	Don't interrupt them.
Be friendly and considerate.	Don't press them to make a decision before they have the chance to explore how they feel about it.
Honor your commitments to them.	Don't put them in a position where they feel taken advantage of or put upon.
Avoid offensive language.	Don't talk down to them or be condescending or patronizing.
Always be polite and respectful.	Don't raise your voice.
Appeal to their need to help.	Don't initiate confrontational conversations.
Actively listen to what they're saying and be mindful of their body language.	Don't treat them impersonally.

How to Speak Yellow	
DOs	**DON'Ts**
Appeal to their need to know and understand.	Don't rush them to make a decision before they have time to think about it.
Appreciate their thoroughness and need for perfection.	Don't present a problem if you don't want them to help solve it.
Appeal to their sense of fairness and personal integrity.	Don't be repetitious.
Use words that mentally stimulate their thinking.	Don't come across as a know-it-all.
Discuss possibilities with them.	Don't ask "Why" questions.
Ask them "What" questions.	Don't become emotional.
Be truthful and honest.	Don't expect them to not challenge what you're saying.
Solicit their suggestions and ideas.	Don't question their logic or imply that they're intellectually flawed.

How to Speak Green	
DOs	**DON'Ts**
Engage them in the conversation by asking for their ideas.	Don't bog them down with details.
Allow the discussion to flow freely.	Don't silence them when they're expressing how they're feeling.
Show interest in them and their ideas.	Don't criticize them or attack them personally.
Appeal to their creativity.	Don't be sarcastic and disrespectful.
Use their name; it's music to their ears and personalizes the conversation.	Don't overwhelm them with rules.
Use metaphors and words that paint pictures.	Don't try to control the conversation.
Allow them to ask questions.	Don't raise your voice or use threatening tones.
Keep conversations light, fun, and lively.	Don't ignore them or what they have to say.

One Last Word

It's important to remember that when we find ourselves caught in a conversation where we don't see eye to eye with someone, we don't underestimate or try to minimize personality differences, because they're by no means inconsequential. They're like a loaded gun ready to go off, and when they do, they can either hit their intended target—meaning that a mutual understanding will be achieved—or they can misfire and cause the people involved to become frustrated and angry or have their feelings hurt. Or, they can miss the mark altogether and totally break down the lines of communication.

This process can be unforgiving because what's spoken verbally or conveyed nonverbally is irreversible and significantly affects whether a bond of trust can be established. Once something hurtful is said, it's difficult to take back the words or mend the emotional wounds that those hurt feelings can create. Therefore, it's important to remember that we must continually take responsibility for our words and be aware of their impact before we express them. If we want someone to trust us with their heart, then it's our responsibility to steer the process so that there's both talking and listening—a mutual interaction that includes the exchange of feelings.

Successful communication is the ability to speak another person's language and put ourselves in their shoes. The ongoing challenge, however, is how to do that without thinking or feeling that we have to compromise ourselves in the process. The solution is to embrace personality differences and make them work for you. The dividends will outweigh the effort, and the return will be mutually beneficial to both parties in the love relationship.

Afterword

The Most Important Love of All

Self-love—it sounds trite, doesn't it? Most people are looking outside of themselves, searching for someone else, who through their love may show them how to care for themselves. Yet I'm sure that at some time we've all been told that we should love ourselves. After all, that's a standard mantra that comes with parenthood, and is part of the wisdom that we're spiritually obligated to share with our children.

Loving ourselves isn't as easy as it sounds, however, because in many cases we haven't been taught how or may not even really understand what it means. Time and time again in the course of my work, people ask me, "Will I ever find true love or the love of my life?" I consistently tell them: "You have. It is you, and it's within you." Then they usually say, "No, that's not what I meant. What I want to know is whether I'll ever find someone who will truly love me." My response is: "Not until you learn to love yourself."

The first step in finding self-love is understanding who you really are and learning to embrace all the qualities that make you unique: your personality color, strengths, talents, weaknesses, quirks, and even those idiosyncrasies that seem to pop up from time to time. What that means is accepting the whole kit and caboodle—the good, the bad, and the ugly. I hope that by now you're beginning to love your personality color and are feeling good about who you are.

The second step in finding self-love is learning how to deal with the people in your life who aren't like you, and doing so in a way that doesn't put you in a position that degrades or devalues who you are. The first step helps you create the love you desire, and the second helps you keep it once you do find it.

Self-Love . . . a Spiritual Metamorphosis

The love of self is different from the love we have for others. It's transformative, healing, and empowers us to reach beyond our self-perceived limitations so that we can do our greatest work—our soul's work. The energy of self-love is the highest vibration of this emotion, and it's meant to deliver us from the conditioning and other people's perceptions that have led us to believe that we're less than who we truly are.

It opens our eyes so that we can see our strengths and natural talents, and it frees our heart so that we can find the love we crave and need so much. Its elegance and grace are just waiting for the opportunity to present themselves and infuse their light into our perception of life. Self-love offers us a sense of a higher purpose and divine connection, and adds meaning to our lives. It calls on us to recast the ideas we have about ourselves and to reinvent who we are through every experience by making different choices, using our reasons and not those of others.

This wonderful affection encompasses an array of behaviors, attitudes, emotions, values, knowledge, and beliefs that are at the core of our essence. Its expression is found through our personality color and the qualities aligned with the inherent traits of that type. Self-love asks that we remove the perceptions that are holding us back and release the habits and comfort zones that have become our masters and that cause us to engage in self-destructive behavior. Every day we must seek to learn new things about ourselves that we've been reluctant to know; expanding our consciousness and creating new thoughts. It will help us find the courage to remove the grip that fear has over our thinking and our emotions, which has dictated how we live our lives.

Self-love asks us to stretch ourselves and move above and beyond our current resting spot. It calls for us to nurture and care for ourselves as we would for others, along with being kind to ourselves and showing the same respect that we show other people. It asks that we be attentive, intuitive, thoughtful, truthful, insightful, and forgiving toward ourselves. It teaches us the fine art of being human and how to fully value and utilize our talents and strengths.

The Importance of Self-Esteem

Self-love is reflected by a healthy self-esteem and is present in our demeanor. Those first few critical seconds of a first impression tell more about how we feel about ourselves than any words can convey. If we're feeling good about who we are, then we come across with a sense of self-confidence and an air of grace. Consequently, people find us appealing and are attracted to us. Conversely, if we aren't happy with who we are, then others will see that, too, and will respond accordingly. Because when we aren't self-confident, we're telling other people that we're insecure, weak, vulnerable, helpless, submissive, inferior, or emotionally flawed. The lack of healthy self-esteem leaves us vulnerable to people who have a need to control, manipulate, and even abuse—those who find pleasure in hurting others, especially those they love.

Self-worth is different from self-esteem because it's established by other people and their ideas about who we are, how they feel about us, and who they think we should be. This assessment distorts the perception we have of ourselves and can negatively influence who we become. It causes us to create artificial behaviors whose primary motivations are to please others, even at our own expense. Self-worth issues open the doors to criticism and personal rejection, and are the main cause of many of the emotional wounds we carry deep inside our heart and in our psyche. These issues prevent us from being and becoming who we really are.

Self-esteem, on the other hand, is how we feel about ourselves. It's self-directed and is created by the positive views we have of ourselves and our personality color. The prime directives of healthy self-esteem are self-love and self-acceptance, with the mission of teaching us how to connect our head and heart to our soul. When this connection is made, we're able to discover our inner spiritual needs.

Self-esteem can't be *created* through the love of others, but it can be *sustained* by their affection. If we're to establish healthy self-esteem, we must do it by ourselves through listening to our heart. This is an easy task for Oranges and Greens, but a difficult one for Reds and Yellows, because it means that they'll have to follow their heart rather than listening to what their head is telling them. A person with healthy self-esteem is proficient in showing themselves the same respect, compassion, patience, and tolerance that they show others. They're the masters of their love destiny, and create the love upon which a solid, enduring relationship can be built.

Self-Love . . . the Catalyst for Human Transformation

Self-love is conscious and supports actively experiencing, enjoying, and participating in the activities of caring, not just going through the motions. By doing this, we're able to find the strength, courage, inspiration, and motivation to move forward on our evolutionary path so that we can learn, grow, change, and evolve. Self-love is what ultimately defines us and sets us apart from everyone else. It's what makes us feel whole and complete. It celebrates change and is forever prodding and nudging us to move forward so that we'll never become stagnant in our behavior or unwilling to engage fully in life and its experiences. Self-love helps release the grip of fear and self-doubt, and moves us into a constant state of becoming, which is the catalyst for human transformation.

The definition of *transformation* is "the process of changing." In the evolutionary process, this is an action stage and must take place before we can rise above and move beyond our current state of being. It offers the greatest opportunity for us to eliminate everything that we believe is holding us back. In return, however, transformation asks a great deal from us, because it requires that we let go of the emotional wounds that we've used (consciously or unconsciously) to protect ourselves from getting hurt. We have to come to terms with how we use thoughts and emotions to sabotage ourselves.

Transformation forces us to venture into the parts of ourselves that feel like a dark side or a shadow and find ways to illuminate them. It asks that we embrace the unknown by providing the vital energy necessary to help us persevere in our quest for greater understanding, and it gives us the courage to face our fears. We must cease blaming others and take responsibility for finding our own self-love as we extract the positive point from the self-worth feedback that we get from others. Transformation purges all concepts that are preventing us from loving ourselves and limiting our personal growth. It liberates us and brings balance and synchronicity back into our lives.

The Law of Magnetic Attraction

There is a saying that "energy flows where intention goes," and this couldn't be truer than in the quest for self-love. How we feel about ourselves is like a boomerang: What we throw out is what comes back to us. If we love ourselves, then others love us back; if we devalue ourselves, then others devalue us. The negative aspect of human nature makes it easy for us to succumb to the temptation to beat ourselves up and say things to and about ourselves that we wouldn't say to our worst enemy. It causes us to sabotage ourselves and participate in self-destructive behavior.

But self-love is a celebration of who we are, and it's one of life's true rewards for all the work we do in seeking to improve ourselves. When we love ourselves, we see that life isn't about blaming ourselves for everything that goes wrong.

Using self-deprecating talk drains us of energy, disconnects us from our soul, and creates false beliefs about what we're capable of accomplishing. It limits how successful we are at finding the love we desire, because it creates erroneous perceptions that we aren't worthy or deserving of being loved. Criticizing our success in love feeds these feelings of unworthiness, and like a self-fulfilling prophecy, this behavior prevents us from finding what we're looking for. It keeps us in a constant state of searching for that perfect person who can save us from ourselves and make the struggles of life seem less burdensome.

As a result, we condone behavior that's manipulative and controlling, and we may put ourselves in relationships that are abusive and emotionally destructive. We do this because we believe that we don't deserve anything better. This happens because we aren't coming from self-love.

When we blame ourselves for things that go wrong, we mentally immobilize ourselves and shut off our positive emotions; rather than seeing solutions, we only see problems. Our ability to draw on our intuition for possibilities and alternatives is shut down, and all we see are the same old choices that we've always made. Remember that all couples have their share of problems; they all fall prey to misunderstandings and disagreements; and everyone has habits, preferences, expectations, and attitudes that affect the quality of their union.

Blaming yourself for what goes wrong doesn't help you or your relationship; it only compounds the problems. Stewing over what happened doesn't make the problem go away, and it brings out the worst patterns in all the personality colors. The reality is that people do things for *their* reasons, not ours, and we aren't responsible for what they do. We're only responsible for ourselves. Focusing endlessly on your faults and weaknesses never improves the situation. This is an important point, especially for the Greens, because they personalize everything and generally see it as being their fault when bad things happen. They believe that if they'd tried harder, said the right thing, or acted differently, then everything would be just fine.

Self-Love . . . the Impact on Health

As a medical intuitive, I've met with hundreds of people who were dealing with life-threatening illnesses, and who came to me to try to understand the deep psychological implications behind their conditions. And while I don't intend to sound judgmental or to minimize what they were experiencing or feeling, I've found that a common denominator across the board was the lack of love—specifically self-love.

Our body is an exquisite machine that's designed to seek homeostasis—that is, a relatively stable state of equilibrium—and to correct any malfunctions that arise over the course of our lives. It even comes equipped with its own inner healer, and when that power is called upon, miracles are known to happen. Yet the key to accessing this inner strength and helping the body remain healthy and balanced lies solely in how we see ourselves.

Understanding personality and working in this field for over 25 years, I've come to know that each of the four colors perceives self-love as differently as they see love itself:

— For the **Reds**, self-love is embracing who they are and learning to mellow out by being less type A. They must let go of the need to control both people and their environment, and learn to play more.

— For **Oranges**, self-love is more difficult to define because they measure themselves based on what they do for others. If I were to ask an Orange what they do for themselves, they'd usually ask, "When?" They see this quality as taking time for themselves and indulging in activities that help them relax and slow down. It's tied to their self-esteem.

— The **Yellows** see self-love as living up to their full potential and making good use of their most valuable asset—their mind. They're happiest when they're thinking and free from any responsibility for the well-being of others. They associate self-love with worthiness.

— For **Greens**, self-love is fleeting. It's like chasing a hat in the wind: They almost catch it, but then it blows away again. This quality is tied to their self-acceptance and is in direct proportion to how they feel about themselves. They experience self-love when they're with someone they care for, but not when there are problems in their relationship. Self-love is present when they're encouraging someone else to follow their dreams, but it disappears when they're not following their own dreams.

Looking to the physical body to help us understand how the lack of self-love affects our health, let me share more about what I've learned as a medical intuitive. The heart, with its four chambers, is one of the few organs that holds both the energies of positive and negative emotions as they pertain to self-love. Depending on how we feel about ourselves at any given moment, it can exacerbate the negative emotions or generate healing energy using positive feelings.

The upper-right chamber (atrium) of the heart is where we carry fear; the lower-right chamber (ventricle) is where we carry anger; the upper-left chamber (atrium) is where we carry the emotional charges associated with betrayal; and the lower-left chamber (ventricle) is where we carry sadness. When we don't love ourselves, all of these emotions are prevalent in our thinking and active in our heart, and they're all significantly impacting the organ's ability to function properly.

However, when we're in a state of self-love, the emotional energy changes and acts as "cancel points," canceling out the ill effects of choosing to see ourselves as less than who we really are—perfect. Self-love sends messages to the brain that all is well, which in turn lets the heart know that we love who we are. This means that the upper-right chamber, rather than being gripped by fear, is full of love; the lower-right chamber, instead of pulsating with anger, experiences compassion; the upper-left chamber is feeling acceptance rather than betrayal; and the lower-left chamber glows with joy instead of sadness.

The Healing Power of Compassion

Compassion is the soul's way of healing our body, mind, and spirit. It begins with a state of grace and ends with self-love. It's one of the soul's highest virtues, and its energy runs throughout our body. In this case, I'm not using the word in the sense of caring feelings that we have for others or what we show other people, and it doesn't mean feeling sorry for someone.

This form of compassion is self-directed, and it comforts us and gives us the courage and strength needed to move forward on our evolutionary journey. It's linked with our inner healer, and its presence fills our heart with hope and our mind with self-loving thoughts. It offers us the opportunity to accept who we are at all times and reminds us that we're always in the right place at the right time. There are no accidents or coincidences.

This quality encompasses forgiveness, and it asks that we pardon ourselves for all the times we believed that we were less than who we really are. Compassion asks us to act as if the bad things we experienced throughout our lives never happened so that we can remove the negative grip they have on us, which is preventing us from caring for ourselves and finding the love we want. It awakens us to our connection to the Divine and helps us hold ourselves in the light. In doing so, we'll see ourselves in an entirely different way—a new, loving, and holistic way.

This compassion requires emotional maturity and the willingness to embrace our shadow and learn to dance with it. It asks that we see ourselves not through our hurts and wounds, but through our accomplishments and achievements. Its energy polishes us, refines our perceptions, and brings forth our inner beauty. It lets us see ourselves through the eyes of the Divine so that we can understand that we're always in a state of becoming one with our higher power. Compassion creates unity with all that exists, and its gifts are self-love, self-esteem, worthiness, and self-acceptance.

The Healing Model of Love

L: Live each day as if it was your first and will be your last.

O: Offer love without expectations or conditions and with an open heart.

V: Value your relationships, for they're life's greatest gifts and your best teachers.

E: Each day, evaluate the patterns of behavior that are holding you back and then change them.

As you finish this book, please remember that we all have a choice in how we see ourselves. It's my hope that in sharing this information, your vision of yourself will be one of self-love, and you'll experience all the love that life has to offer.

A Note of Gratitude

Love is expressed many ways and comes from many sources. This book is a reflection of both. John Donne wrote, "No man is an island," and this is also true of the creation of a book: It's never done by one person. It's the result of contributions by many people. This work has been five years in the making and has over 25 years of research behind it, so it's difficult to recognize all the people who lovingly contributed to it, and who through their stories and struggles taught me about love. I send all of you my love.

My heartfelt gratitude to each and every person who sat across from me in counseling sessions and who attended workshops; to my students at the Ritberger Institute; and all of you who allowed me to ask those difficult questions about love, sex, intimacy, commitment, and passion.

Thank you to my family: my husband, Bruce; Diana Haas; Cynthia Ritberger-Franke; and Brian Ritberger for showing me unconditional love and putting up with all the times when I was stressed and pressed writing this book, and when I was less than loving. Bruce, thank you for all of your support, for your proofreading over and over again, for nudging and pressing me to think out of the box, and for encouraging me to march to my own drummer. I wouldn't be where I am without you or your love. Diana, the moment I looked into your eyes on the day that you were born, I knew what true love really meant. Every day you remind me of that when we have our long-distance coffee together, and I hear your smiling voice on the phone. Cynthia, when I watch you love, nurture, and care tirelessly for your family, I am in awe as to how one person can have so much love in her heart. I could say that it's because you're an Orange, and it's your job. However, it's really because love and loving others is who you really are.

If we really want to know what love is all about, look to the children—in my case, my beautiful granddaughters: Brandi, Jennifer, Taylor, Christy, and Ashley. They love us for who we are, and remind us that when we get too serious about love or life, we need to lighten up, laugh, and have fun—just hang out together.

To my parents, Mary and P.G. Biano. Thanks for all the love you gave me, and yes, even for those times of tough love. Ginger Tharp, aka Sis, thanks for the loads of sisterly love we share. Petty Biano, the lover of life, play, and golf—thanks for reminding me not to take myself so seriously.

Love also comes from those who encourage you to write your books and live your dreams. Thank you Louise L. Hay, Reid Tracy, and all the wonderful people at Hay House, Inc. I'm grateful for being included in your family, and honored to be a part of an organization that's dedicated to publishing mindful, innovative, and inspirational books that can help people change their lives. Jill Kramer, you're an editor extraordinaire, as are Shannon Littrell and Jessica Vermooten. The publicity crew is a joy to work with, always finding creative ways to spread the words of Hay House authors. Thanks, Jacqui Clark.

Danny Levin, what can I say, but I love you. Thank you for all that you've done for me and for being the catalyst for making my dreams come true. You hold a special place in my heart.

Bibliography

Avila, Alexander, *LoveTypes*, NY, Avon Books, 1999

Bear, Mark, Barry Connors & Michael Paradiso, *Neuroscience: Exploring the Brain,* Williams and Wilkins Press, 1996

Baines, John, *The Science of Love,* NY, The John Baines Institute, Inc., 1998

Carter, Rita, *Exploring Consciousness,* Berkeley and Los Angeles, CA, University of California Press, 2002

——, *Mapping the Mind,* Berkeley and Los Angeles, CA, University of California Press, 1999

Frankl, Viktor, *Man's Search for Meaning,* NY, Touchstone, Simon & Schuster, 1984

Gurdjieff, G. I., *Views from the Real World,* NY, E. P. Dutton, 1973

Gurian, Michael, *What Could He Be Thinking?,* NY, St. Martin's Press, 2003

Hardy Jones, Jane & Ruth Sherman, *Intimacy and Type,* Gainesville, FL, Center for Applications of Psychological Type, Inc., 1997

Jung, C. G., *Psychology and Alchemy.* In *Collected Works,* vol. 12. Translated by R. F. C. Hull, Princeton, NJ, Princeton University Press, 1953

——, *Symbols of Transformation.* In *Collected Works,* vol. 5. Translated by R. F. C. Hull, Princeton, NJ, Princeton University Press, 1956

——, *The Structure and Dynamics of the Psyche*. In *Collected Works*, vol. 8. Translated by R. F. C. Hull, Princeton, NJ, Princeton University Press, 1960

——, *The Symbolic Life*. In *Collected Works*, vol. 18. Translated by R. F. C. Hull, Princeton, NJ, Princeton University Press, 1976

——, *Man and His Symbols*, NY, Dell Publishing Co. Inc., 1964

——, *Psychological Types*. In *Collected Works*, vol. 6. Translated by R. F. C. Hull, Princeton NJ, Princeton University Press, 1971

Kingma, Daphne Rose, *True Love*, NY, MJF Books, 1994

Kornfield, Jack, *A Path with Heart*, NY, Bantam Books, 1993

Kroeger, Otto & Janet M. Thuesen, *16 Ways to Love Your Lover*, NY, Delacorte Press, 1994

Levine, Stephen and Ondrea, *Embracing the Beloved*, NY, Doubleday, 1994

Littauer, Florence, *Personality Plus for Couples*, Grand Rapids, MI, Fleming H Revell, 2001

Oldham, John M. & Lois B. Morris, *Personality Self-Portrait*, NY, Bantam Books, 1990

Psaris, Jett & Marlena S. Lyons, *Undefended Love*, Oakland, CA, New Harbinger Publications, Inc., 2000

Quenk, Alex & Naomi, *True Loves*, Palo Alto, Davies-Black Publishing, 1997

Regan, Pamela, *The Mating Game*, Thousand Oaks, CA, Sage Publications, Inc., 2003

Ritberger, Carol, *The Evolutionary Personality: Connecting the Soul with the Human Psyche.* Module Two, Sacramento, CA, The Ritberger Institute, 2001

——, *The Effects of Emotions, Attitudes and Beliefs on Health.* Module Six, Sacramento, CA, The Ritberger Institute, 2002

——, *The Role of Personality in Sickness and in Health,* Module Eight, Sacramento, CA, The Ritberger Institute, 2001

——, *The Art and Science of Intuitive Medicine,* Module Seven, Sacramento, CA, The Ritberger Institute, 2002

——, *Your Personality, Your Health,* Carlsbad, CA, Hay House, Inc., 1998

——, *What Color Is Your Personality?* Carlsbad, CA, Hay House, Inc. 2000

Singer, I., *The Nature of Love,* Chicago, The University of Chicago Press, 1987

——, *The Pursuit of Love,* Baltimore, MD, The Johns Hopkins University Press, 1988

Tieger, Paul and Barbara Barron-Tieger, *Just Your Type*, NY, Little, Brown & Company, 2000

About the Author

Carol Ritberger, Ph.D., medical intuitive, is an innovative leader in the fields of personality typology and intuitive medicine. She has devoted more than 25 years to researching the impact of stress, emotions, and personality type on the health and well-being of the physical body. Carol holds two doctorates, one in religious philosophy and the other in esoteric philosophy and hermetic sciences. She's the author of *Your Personality, Your Health* and *What Color is Your Personality?* both of which have received national recognition for their innovative approach to self-help. Her work has been featured in *Good Housekeeping, Yoga Journal, Woman's World, Intuition Magazine,* and *New Age Journal.* She has appeared on television programs such as *Extra, Healthy Living,* and *New Attitudes,* as well as many national radio programs.

Carol is the executive director of The Ritberger Institute, which offers personal and professional development programs. The goal of the institute is to assist its students in accessing and developing their intuition for business, personal, and spiritual growth. It offers an array of classes, including personality training and certification and intuitive-medicine programs. Carol's personal goal is to influence the way that allopathic medicine approaches the diagnostic and healing processes by bringing to it skilled and experienced intuitive diagnosticians and holistic-practitioner professionals.

Carol lives in Northern California, with her husband, Bruce, with whom she cofounded The Ritberger Institute.

For more information on programs and presentations offered through The Ritberger Institute, please visit her Website: **www.ritberger.com.**

Notes

Notes

We hope you enjoyed this Hay House book.
If you'd like to receive a free catalog featuring additional
Hay House books and products, or if you'd like information
about the Hay Foundation, please contact:

Hay House, Inc.
P.O. Box 5100
Carlsbad, CA 92018-5100

(760) 431-7695 or (800) 654-5126
(760) 431-6948 (fax) or (800) 650-5115 (fax)
www.hayhouse.com

Published and distributed in Australia by: Hay House Australia Pty.
Ltd. • 18/36 Ralph St. • Alexandria NSW 2015 • *Phone:* 612-9669-4299 •
Fax: 612-9669-4144 • www.hayhouse.com.au

Published and distributed in the United Kingdom by: Hay House UK,
Ltd. • Unit 62, Canalot Studios • 222 Kensal Rd., London W10 5BN •
Phone: 44-20-8962-1230 • *Fax:* 44-20-8962-1239 • www.hayhouse.co.uk

Published and distributed in the Republic of South Africa by:
Hay House SA (Pty), Ltd., P.O. Box 990, Witkoppen 2068 •
Phone/Fax: 27-11-706-6612 • orders@psdprom.co.za

Distributed in Canada by: Raincoast • 9050 Shaughnessy St., Vancouver, B.C. V6P 6E5 • *Phone:* (604) 323-7100 • *Fax:* (604) 323-2600

Tune in to **www.hayhouseradio.com**™ for the best in inspirational
talk radio featuring top Hay House authors! And, sign up via the Hay
House USA Website to receive the Hay House online newsletter and
stay informed about what's going on with your favorite authors. You'll
receive bimonthly announcements about: Discounts and Offers, Special
Events, Product Highlights, Free Excerpts, Giveaways, and more!
www.hayhouse.com